Praise fo

"I remember the first time I heard Jay Wentz share this message. It was a decade ago in our backyard in San Diego, next to a cobbled-together half-pipe, to a rough and, on any other day, disrespectful bunch of young surfers.

"His passion was contagious. They were enthralled, as you will be. That is, if you're ready to listen and honestly come face-to-face with the gnarliest question of all— 'Am I ready to die?'!

"Spoiler alert: only when we can answer this question with an emphatic 'Yes!' will we be ready to *truly live*. Full-on. As God planned for us all along.

"My mate Jay, in this gritty and intriguing guide for even the jaded, post-truth, world-weary traveler, points us to a fresh hope. He persuasively argues that, despite even (and this is wild!) *through* the toughest parts of our lives, God is shaping us and revealing Himself to us in preparation for an epic eternity with Him. I challenge you to listen and take action. The alternative is way worse than any of us could imagine, and yet God's invitation to each of us is way better than we deserve."

Rev. Nic Gilmour
Co-lead pastor of Goodlife Community Church, Sunshine Coast, Australia, and board member of Christian Surfers International

"What can I say except to let others know there are not enough complimentary adjectives to describe how much I enjoyed *Are You Ready?* by Jay Wentz.

"It took me a while to read this wonderful book because on more than one occasion I had to stop, go back, and re-read a section. On other occasions, the Holy Spirit encouraged me to stop and reflect on my own life, sometimes bringing me to tears.

"That said, *Are You Ready?* deeply nourishes the soul, calling to mind the African-American spiritual, 'There is a balm in Gilead, to make the wounded whole. There is a balm in Gilead to heal the sin-sick soul.'

"*Are You Ready?* can be a valuable aid to pastors, preachers, counselors, and everyone simply in love with God, helping them grow in His love and become true messengers of the Good News. This masterpiece comes from the beautiful heart and soul of the author and will touch many hearts."

MONSIGNOR DENNIS MIKULANIS
Founding Member of the San Diego Regional Interfaith Collaborative

"The question is simple, but the answer is paramount. *Are You Ready?* is the most compelling account of my need for Christ's salvation that I have ever read.

"Having survived many perilous moments as a US Navy SEAL over the past twenty years, Jay Wentz offers a deeply relatable book that reaffirms what matters in this life and in eternity. I can't recommend *Are You Ready?* enough."

COMMANDER PETE CHAMIS
US Navy SEAL

"*Are You Ready?* is a meaningful, engaging read that gets you thinking about what it really looks like to be ready to meet Jesus, while also making the most of your life today. Author Jay Wentz invites you to reflect and wrestle more deeply with what it means to be truly ready."

"Jay also brings Scripture to life in a relatable way, mixing in real stories and practical takeaways you can actually use. *Are You Ready?* is encouraging, challenging, and helpful, all at the same time."

TROY MARTIN
Lead Pastor of Venture Church, Encinitas, California

"At Billabong, we came up with the slogan, 'Only a Surfer Knows the Feeling.' Don't get me wrong, I love surfing—the freedom, the communion with nature, the stoke—but this too shall pass. So what's on the 'other side?' Here's my answer: 'Only a Person Who Falls in Love with Jesus Knows the Feeling.'

In *Are You Ready?,* Jay Wentz unpacks and explores this slogan I've coined from the vantage point of the Bible and what Jesus has to say about being prepared and being good stewards of our time here on earth. I'm mindful of what Jesus says in Revelation 3:20 (NIV): 'Here I am! I stand at the door and knock. If anyone hears my voice and opens the door, I will come in and eat with that person, and they with me.'

"I encourage you to open the door, break bread with Jesus, and be transformed by reading this highly personal, thought-provoking, but ultimately practical book."

JOE KNOERNSCHILD (aka Joe K.)
Co-Founder of Billabong USA and Hurley International

ARE YOU READY?

Are You Ready? Living a Life That Matters—Today and in the Afterlife

ISBN: 979-8-9990457-2-0 (paperback), 979-8-9990457-3-7 (hardcover)

Printed in the United States of America

Published by Turning Page Books

Editorial assistance by Mike Yorkey (mikeyorkey.com)

Cover and interior design by Emily Morelli (bluemusestudio.com)

To contact Jay Wentz, write him at jay@jcgdev.com or call or text him at 858-204-5438. Please visit his website at AreYouReadyforJesus.com.

ARE YOU READY?

Living a Life That Matters—
Today and in the Afterlife

Jay Wentz
with Mike Yorkey

Turning Page
BOOKS

Contents

"Readiness means a right relationship to God and a knowledge of where we are at present . . . readiness for God means we are ready for the tiniest little thing or the great big thing . . . it makes no difference . . . Be ready for the sudden surprise visits of God. A ready person never needs to get ready."

Oswald Chambers
My Utmost for His Highest

This is the spectacular view from our vacation home on a prominent headland on Point Conception, north of Santa Barbara County, Central California. A windy, two-lane dirt road gave us access to a remote beach, where I loved to surf and take long, secluded walks with my family.

Introduction

by Jay Wentz

It all began on an early morning search for surf a bit north of Point Conception, a rugged point of land that juts out where the north end of the Santa Barbara Channel meets the open Pacific Ocean in Central California. My family and I shared a vacation house with some friends that sat atop one of the highest hills and afforded us a view of the remote and sparsely populated landscape between our home and the coastline.

With our surfboards tucked in the back of my dated and dented Toyota Land Cruiser, my good buddy Benji and I bounced along a bumpy dirt road, careful not to spill our hot, steaming coffee.

Behind us, a gorgeous sun had crested the Santa Ynez mountains on a clear, cold Sunday morning in early January 2007. The lack of wind portended glassy conditions in frigid water no warmer than 54 degrees and likely colder. Along with a full wetsuit, we were prepared to don a neoprene hoodie, booties, and gloves.

But surfing wasn't the only thing I was marinating on that morning. As the caffeine kicked in, I blurted a question that came out of left field: "Hey, Benji. Are you ready to die today?"

My friend of some twenty-plus years nearly choked on his coffee. "Where the heck did that come from?" he wondered.

"I don't know. Pretty random, huh?"

I thought about my question all weekend but couldn't find any satisfactory answers. Sure, I had many discussions with good friends and family members over the years, high on the ranch hill, about the greatness of God and His magnificent creation. But on that particular morning, I had asked perhaps the most crucial question of all: *Was I ready to die that day?* And if I did happen to perish, was I prepared to meet the God of the Universe, the One who created me in His image and likeness?

On one level, I believed I would stand face-to-face with the One who made me when that moment arrived. But did I really understand what it meant to be *ready* for my day of death? Was I prepared to "meet my Maker" as so many say?

You may have had similar thoughts. If you have, then questions like these may have entered your consciousness:

- What does getting ready to meet God entail?
- What does adequate preparation look like?
- What does it take to live a life of readiness before meeting our Creator?

The quest to find answers—something that has consumed my thoughts for nearly twenty years—is what *Are You Ready?* is all about.

If you're a surfer like I am, you've probably seen *Step Into Liquid*, a movie that includes scenes of extreme thrill-seekers being towed into gigantic 100-foot waves at Cortes Banks, 110 miles off the California coast west of San Diego.[1]

The massive waves are so tall, so fast, and so gnarly that I have to imagine that any surfer willing to drop in on a wave the size of a ten-story building has to be consumed with this thought as a jet ski tows him into position:

Am I ready to die?

What about you? Sure, you're not taking a boat to Cortes Banks or paddling out to the giant waves found at Jaws off the coast of Maui or at Mavericks next to Santa Cruz in Northern California. Your idea of risk may be becoming a lifelong Chicago Cubs fan. But consider all the tragedies we hear about nearly every day—e-bikers losing their lives when hit by a distracted driver, those who die in split-second car crashes, innocent victims of an active shooter in the workplace, and those who perish from drownings, falls, and heart attacks. Each of them likely woke up that morning with nary a consideration that this would be the last time they witnessed the dawning of a new day.

Much of our earthly time goes into preparing for life's many varied experiences. If one is a thinking person, then one should be concerned about being adequately prepared.

As I've thought about meeting God face-to-face since my surfing trip to Point Conception, it has become clear how brief life is compared to eternity.

I believe the most consequential event we must prepare for is closing our eyes for the final time here on planet Earth and opening them on the other side when we stand before Jesus Christ.

Now, you may not believe things will happen that way. You may not be sure there is an afterlife, or perhaps you're on the

---

1 If you would like to see how big these massive waves really are, go to YouTube and use these search words: 100-foot waves Cortes Banks.

fence but open to the idea. Wherever you are, it would be good to think about what happens when you take your last breath. Have you given any thought to what happens when you die?

Our popular culture does not like to hear or address that question. In fact, our present-day society works overtime to distract us from facing such a critical and essential inquiry. We're told to dream as if we have forever but live for today.

I believe that when the most significant decisions of your life loom, you should give careful thought to the preparation for and the consequences of those decisions, especially when it comes to being ready to meet God. So let me ask you this as we move forward:

- Are you ready to be all you can be?
- Are you ready for genuine relationships?
- Are you ready to view your work life differently?
- Are you ready to show up and display the Divinity that dwells within you?
- Are you ready to experience a peace that passes all understanding?
- Are you ready to forgive yourself and others freely?
- Are you ready to see others as Jesus sees them?
- Are you ready to see yourself as Jesus sees you?
- Are you ready to be more childlike in your approach to life?

These were some of the questions I began asking myself after driving to a favorite surf spot on an early January morning. Little did I know that God would test my understanding of readiness within a year in the closest and most personal of ways.

Early in 2008, the Great Recession was upon us. The economic slump began when the U.S. housing market went from boom to bust. Mortgage-backed securities lost significant value, and the real estate market tanked.

I happened to be in the real estate game at the time. I was an owner and managing partner of a large hotel renovation project in the San Diego area that was in serious trouble because of the suddenly depressed economy. I had done nothing incorrectly or foolishly, but pretty much everything my wife, Catherine, and I had worked for was at risk because of this one project.

Nobody has to remind me that I married up when Catherine and I tied the knot in 1991. She has filled my life with great joy and brought out the best in me. I'm not sure what I did to deserve a wife as kind, smart, and beautiful—inside and out—as she is.

Was I ready for what God had in store for us?

During this tremendously stressful and challenging time, I have an exact moment etched in my mind while praying with a pastor friend. He asked me to open my hands and stretch them out, palms up.

Then he prayed out loud that God would solve the business problem in my life and that I would, at a deep level, recognize that every situation God gives us in life needs to be treated with hands out, palms up and open, because God gives and God takes away for His greater purposes. I did this even though, at that moment, what God was doing didn't make any sense to me.

Here's what happened after that prayer: things got worse. In November 2008, my precious wife of seventeen years suddenly developed flu-like symptoms.[2]

Then her condition worsened—rapidly. Within three days, she was admitted to the intensive care unit at Scripps Hospital in La Jolla, fifteen miles north of San Diego. Her organs were shutting down, and her bodily systems were crumbling into sepsis.

Doctors theorized that she could have been one of the first cases of swine flu, but they weren't sure because the first doctor who had seen her had not cultured her blood but instead had given her an antibiotic.

Her life hung in the balance. Catherine was put on life support and placed into a medically induced coma to save her life. A team of infectious disease specialists was brought in, dozens of blood cultures were done, and seven of the most powerful antibiotics were pumped into her system twenty-four hours a day.

Hundreds, perhaps thousands, of prayers were raised by scores of people who knew Catherine from her many years in children's ministry at our church and in her counseling ministry.

And still, she failed to rally. On Thanksgiving Day 2008, two of

2 When Catherine and I married in 1991, I became the stepfather of her two children from a previous marriage: Amber, seventeen, and Michael, thirteen. Catherine and I would later have a daughter together in 1993, whom we named Georgiana.

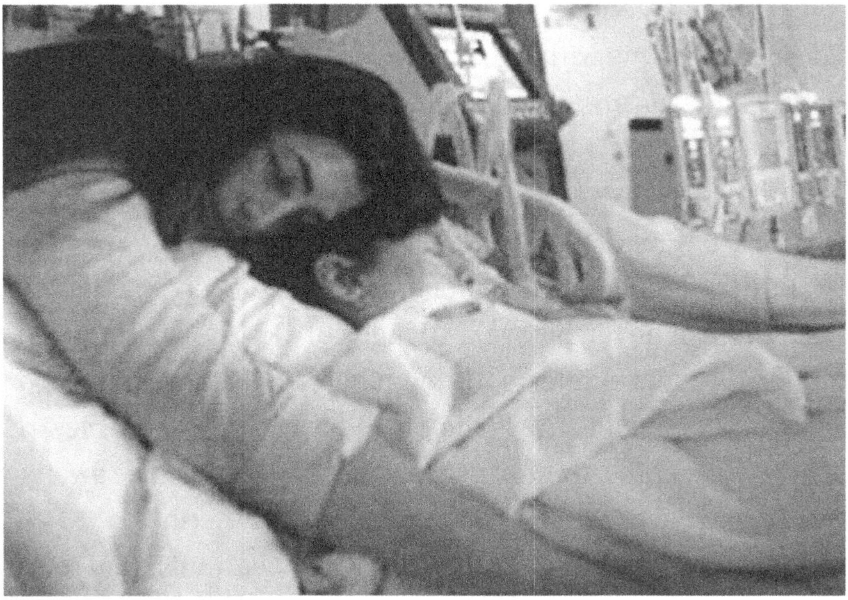

We didn't know if we would lose Catherine when she fought for her life in the ICU. Flu-like symptoms developed into a life-threatening situation: her organs shut down, she was intubated and placed into a medically induced coma, and her immune system mounted an extreme response to an infection, producing a condition known as sepsis. She was hospitalized for seventeen days.

Amber's extraordinary devotion to her mother—through countless hours of bedside vigils, comforting her and praying over her, as well as her many astute and pointed conversations with the physicians—was Christlike love exemplified.

my three children, Amber and Michael, and I were told by doctors that we might very well lose her that night.

I had a bed in the ICU that I would use to grab a little sleep here and there. Amber and Michael were momentarily outside the ICU.

As I lay down in the dim light on that Thanksgiving evening, I heard occasional beeping from the digital medical devices connected to her. I felt a foreboding in the darkness, along with deep distress. Unable to sleep, I pulled myself out of bed, knelt at Catherine's bedside, and wept. I couldn't imagine losing her.

Then I prayed, "God, please spare her life."

At that moment, as her life hung in the balance, I heard God's voice speak to me with unmistakable clarity: *Jay, are you ready to give me your precious Catherine?*

I was startled. I had never heard the audible voice of God before.

I said out loud, "No, Lord, I'm not ready."

But then, in an eternal moment, a peace overcame me and filled me like never before. I thought of God's own Son in the garden of Gethsemane on the night before His crucifixion. Even though He prayed to the Father, "Let this cup pass from me," He willingly accepted the torture, shame, and death that awaited him. Could I accept what could happen to Catherine?

I realized I had to trust the Lord wholeheartedly, regardless of my feelings. With tears streaming down my face, I whispered in my own still, small voice, "Father, may Your will, not mine, be done."

Before dawn, Amber, Michael, and I met in the hospital cafeteria, which was quiet and still. I lay my head down at a table and thought about what the day might bring.

I did not know what to make of the whole situation except that the thought of possibly losing my wife was incomprehensible. I opened my eyes and stared at the ordinary cafeteria tabletop. I saw something in the design. Around the table's edge were small inlaid tiles in the shape of white doves.

Wow, Lord. Even amid such great sadness and turmoil, You let me know You are here. Thank You.

That very morning, Catherine's condition miraculously improved. Two days later, her breathing tube was removed, and she was slowly brought out of the coma.

The doctors told us she would make it, but full recovery would be a long road back.

Catherine did recover, although the process took longer than expected. Unfortunately, my wife never fully regained the same excellent health she had before contracting the disease, which doctors ended up diagnosing as Acute Respiratory Distress Syndrome (ARDS).

Some eighteen years later, I can safely say that this experience forever changed my family and me. I have been challenged to live a more robust life of readiness ever since. As part of that effort, I've completed *Are You Ready?* with the hope and a prayer that this book will challenge you to meaningfully confront critical life situations where readiness is key because the impact on you and others is significant. Look at this effort as an average man or woman's guide to navigating and applying the gospel of peace. I am very much that average man!

In the pages ahead, I will take you through a discussion of readiness questions and applicable principles incorporating Scripture at its base, as well as points of view from the secular world. I will bring my life experiences and other stories together in a way that will encourage and challenge you to live a life worth living so that you will be ready to meet God at any moment.

For those still unsure where you stand with God, I invite you to hang in there and consider the ideas I share in an unpredictable world shaped by self-gratification, self-redemption, conflict, war, uncertainty, and disease. Are you ready to think about what lies ahead and whether there's something far greater for you to consider in your life?

I hope so. Let me share a great Scripture that fits what I'm trying to say, and it comes from Luke 12:40 (NLT):

> You also must be ready all the time, for the Son of Man will come when least expected.

So let me ask you this: ***Are you ready?***

1

Where Are We Now?

A wise person thinks a lot about death,
while a fool thinks only about
having a good time.

—Ecclesiastes 7:4 (NLT)

"It's not that I'm afraid to die. I just don't
want to be there when it happens."

—Filmmaker Woody Allen

The substance of *Are You Ready?* can be hemmed in by two bookends.

One bookend is: "If you thought this life would be easy, you might want to change your thinking."

The second bookend is this: "If you want to end up on your deathbed with as few regrets as possible, then learn that a life of true and valuable meaning is not about what you acquire but about what you receive and give away to others."

My goal is to give you some thoughts on transitioning from the first bookend to the second before drawing your last breath.

I feel a sense of urgency because our crazy world is changing so quickly. People are much more uncertain and afraid of their futures because of the continual political strife and conflicts tearing our country apart.

Guess what? Notwithstanding all the "big" issues facing us as a country, we can do little to control what's happening beyond our front doors. (A small sigh of relief may be appropriate here.) All we can do is control our actions and our reactions to life's circumstances by taking one day at a time and doing our best to live a rich life filled with meaning and purpose, including being part of causes we are passionate about.

One of the few positive things we can say about the last half-dozen years is that many of us have had to think much more about what's essential in life, which has shifted our focus accordingly. During this time of introspection, you may ask yourself questions like:

- Who can be trusted?
- What can I depend on these days?
- What can I latch onto that has true meaning and enduring strength?

We've seen how people latch onto social media portals like Facebook, Instagram, TikTok, and X, news aggregator sites (Politico and Daily Kos on the left and Citizen Free Press and DailyWire on the right, to name just a couple), and cable news (CNN and MS Now, formerly MSNBC, on the left and Fox News on the right) in recent years.

Since most of us no longer get our news from the morning newspaper or evening television broadcasts, we engorge ourselves with an endless buffet of digital, TV, and radio news, commentary, and podcasts from various sources with vastly different levels of accuracy and perspectives. While it's often hard to separate the wheat of truth from the chaff of disinformation, it's also easy to get sucked into the political battles of the day and let the walls go up between family, friends, and neighbors.

I raise these points because I'm as guilty as anyone of getting caught up in the cares of the world. But looking around me and noticing how people increasingly anesthetize themselves with drinking, drugs, sex, Amazon purchases, and streaming videos because of what the world is throwing at them daily, I wonder how many are questioning the meaning of life. Are they perhaps considering their mortality for the first time? Are you?

For many years, I have believed in Jesus as the second member of the Holy Trinity, the creator of the universe, and the God who became a man and walked the planet just like us. I understand the leap of faith required to cross over from Jesus being a good teacher or prophet to Someone who explicitly said who He was—the God of the Universe who became human to rescue us from our failings, sin, and eternal death.

No other religion on the planet has its primary architect claiming to be God in the flesh. Every religion other than Christianity has a set of rules for the devoted to becoming "worthy" of a seat at God's table, worthy of elevating oneself to a "better" state of mind, or worthy of having a more enjoyable place after death. Only Christianity proclaims a God who reaches down from the heavens to touch mankind authentically and personally. His sacrifice on the Cross at Calvary offers eternal peace with Him by a simple act of faith and humble acceptance of His unmerited gift of grace.

In this book, you will unequivocally understand my devotion to Jesus Christ, but it's okay if you are not yet a follower of

Jesus. I just ask that you be open to Jesus and His teachings and see where that may lead you. There are many books about Jesus—in addition to the Bible—that pass with flying colors all the accepted modes of literary historical authentication and accuracy. These resources attest to the birth of Jesus, His life and teachings, the miracles He performed, and His death and Resurrection.

I want to expose you to Jesus, the everlasting God, and Jesus the man. Perhaps after considering His approaches to life's daily issues and His ideas on being ready for the kingdom of God in the hereafter, it's time to take a deeper look at this most incredible Being. His teaching on living a life of true value and meaning hasn't been replicated or superseded since.

Here's a major point: If our global leaders followed His teachings, then this world would be a much better place for us all.

Perhaps you will come to a point where I was many years ago and submit to His authority and Lordship over your life . . . or perhaps not. Eventually, we all need to decide what to do with Jesus and judge for ourselves whether He was a liar, a lunatic, or Lord of all, as British lay theologian C.S. Lewis said many years ago.

Jesus doesn't allow us to place Him on a shelf as only a great teacher or prophet alongside many other teachers and prophets throughout history. He did not give us that option. He declared Himself to be God incarnate, so everyone should carefully consider His words and actions, along with the historical validations for them. We want to be ready for what will happen when we close our eyes for the final time and cross over to the afterlife.

I heard a story about a pastor who was having dinner with a friend who did not consider Jesus to be anything more than a great teacher.

The pastor patiently listened to his friend make his case and then had this to say: "When I die, and it turns out I am right for believing in the deity of Jesus, then my life here on earth has not been impaired in any material way," the pastor said. "I would put forth that my life, while replete with human failures, has been rich and helpful to others while trying to live out Jesus' principles in good times and challenging times. If I am wrong about Jesus, it won't matter because I'll be dust. But if it turns out you're wrong about Jesus, then you gambled on where you'll end up for eternity, which, the last time I checked, is an incredibly long time. That would be quite a large gamble to lose."

A friend reminded me that this life is as bad as it gets for Christians. For those who don't believe, this life is as good as it gets. That's certainly something to ponder when one thinks beyond the confines of earthly time, such as thinking through what happens when we die. We don't know whether our stay on Earth will be brief, extended, or in between, but it will certainly be one of those. At some moment in your life—I hope right now—you will ask yourself these questions:

- What am I here for?
- What's the point of living?
- How do I successfully and meaningfully navigate relationships with others?
- How can I best overcome life's challenges?
- How do I finish well?

From the moment a person is born, he or she is headed toward a date with death. No one likes to contemplate this reality, and most human beings do everything possible to shield themselves from this or diminish or deny its momentousness. Even though no one desires to spend any time thinking about the inevitability of death, it seems like now would be an excellent time to consider what happens when we die and, therefore, how we should live when we are alive.

I was reminded of how the world seeks to distract us from what's really important when I watched the 2020 movie *The Social Dilemma*. The docudrama does a deep dive into how the people behind social media websites and apps like Facebook and Instagram use manipulative techniques to keep us on their platforms and develop an actual psychological addiction to social media. Undoubtedly, the gusher of alerts and "likes" from social media portals is relentless.

Social media is like a dog chasing its tail—there's never a satisfactory ending. Our fleshly desires can never be satiated. That's why we crave endless notifications about the number of "likes" on our posts or the availability of new comments to read. We're learning that Big Tech companies, which amass incredible amounts of personal data, are getting better and better at manipulating users and influencing our behavior so they can profit. If you have a Facebook account, your personal data is typically worth more than $30 of advertising revenue to Facebook in any given quarter.

Life outside of social media is worth far more than thirty bucks a quarter, and it should be since each human life is richly unique and should be acknowledged as such. When lived honestly and meaningfully, our lives are a sequence of choices, actions, and reactions: our hearts beget thoughts, our thoughts beget actions, our actions beget habits, and our habits become our character.

This is the irrefutable human way. We may think we can avoid this cosmic sequencing, but eventually, our actions are our legacy, and our habits reveal to others who we are, even when we think nobody is looking. In a rapidly changing world, we have a proverbial "once-in-a-lifetime chance" to leave a legacy that transcends time. That legacy may be known by many or may only impact your immediate family and a close circle of friends who will never forget you or your honest and encouraging actions, thoughts, and words. The Jesus I serve is interested in the quality of your heart, not the quantity of "likes" by others.

You still have time to design and navigate a course of action and reactions that will lead to a life of real meaning and purpose. That should be your goal. If there's anything we've learned since 2020, it's that we all need to be ready for the unexpected because we control very little besides our actions toward others and our reactions to life's events.

Yes, I am a sold-out follower of Jesus Christ.

Yes, I love Jesus Christ more every day because of what He did for me.

This book will reflect my beliefs about Jesus and His approaches to life's pressing questions of readiness—and compare them to the world's approaches. Jesus walked the desert sands of modern-day Israel two thousand years ago. He was fully human yet also fully God, as evidenced by His sinless life and the abundance of miracles, including His resurrection from the dead. He lived the life we should live, and He paid the ultimate price that we should have paid by dying to reconcile us with God so that we can have an eternal relationship with Him, the Father, and the Holy Spirit.

Rising from the grave and conquering death was witnessed by hundreds and should give us abundant hope for what is coming for those who believe in His name and follow Him. I hope and pray that—as you see His way of dealing with life— you will consider Jesus at a deeper level and be drawn to Him.

2

Are You Ready to Meet the One Who Made You?

"I am ready to meet my Maker. Whether my Maker is prepared for the great ordeal of meeting me is another matter."

—Winston Churchill, Prime Minister of Great Britain during World War II

To say you're ready for something implies some level of preparation for an action or event that you're prepared to undertake.

I'm assuming that you believe or might believe that Jesus is God, or perhaps you believe in the concept of a Supreme Being, but not Jesus as God. Wherever you are on the spiritual spectrum, I want you to *assume*, for the sake of this chapter, that Jesus *is* God and there is a God who created you and loves you unconditionally. Not only do you believe in Him, but you have faith you will meet Him one day.

As you consider what you might do to prepare for that

"crossover" on your appointed day of death and meeting God face to face, it's essential to consider what God has to say about the matter of preparation directly *and* indirectly. You might want to bear in mind whether what God needs from you is being addressed, so let me start with this question:

What is most important to God?

One answer is found in Luke 10:27 (ESV) when Jesus said:

> "You shall love the Lord your God with all your heart and with all your soul and with all your strength and with all your mind, and your neighbor as yourself."

That Scripture verse describes God's order of priorities and emphasizes the importance of loving God, which comes through knowing Him rather than performing for Him. In Matthew 7:21-23 (NLT), He speaks about those who will appear before Him someday, claiming to have been believers during their time on Earth:

> "Not everyone who calls out to me, 'Lord! Lord!' will enter the Kingdom of Heaven. Only those who actually do the will of my Father in heaven will enter. On judgment day many will say to me, 'Lord! Lord! We prophesied in your name and cast out demons in your name and performed many miracles in your name.' But I will reply, 'I never knew you. Get away from me, you who break God's laws.'"

Yikes! Jesus' statement has always been frightening and sobering for me to consider. I realized Jesus was speaking to those who claimed they were followers of Him and were sure they were doing what was necessary to meet Him, but they really weren't. They didn't realize life wasn't about earning their way into God's favor. Instead, God's greatest desire was for them to truly know Him as part of realizing they were made in His image (Genesis 1:26).

So, how do you ensure you're *not* one of those whom Jesus says, "I never knew you"?

Answer: by staying consistently close to Him, and you do that by starting each waking day with reading His Word, praying with a recommitted and submissive heart to His Lordship, and trusting Him, no matter what.

After all, He created us! He has our best interests in mind, knows everything, is perfect, and will never lie to us so that you can live each day fully without anxiety about the future or your inevitable meeting with God. We are to abide in Him:

> "Abide in me, and I in you. As the branch cannot bear fruit by itself, unless it abides in the vine, neither can you, unless you abide in me. I am the vine; you are the branches. Whoever abides in me and I in him, he it is that bears much fruit, for apart from me you can do nothing."
>
> —JOHN: 15:4-5 (ESV)

Compared to eternity, our lives on planet Earth are very, very short. You can grasp this idea metaphorically by imagining you are holding a long rope, marked with a half inch of blue tape at its beginning. The rope extends from where you're sitting and goes out the front door, to the sidewalk, and down the street as far as the eye can see—and way beyond that. In essence, that rope literally goes on forever.

The rope represents eternity, but your lifetime is like the half inch of blue tape at the beginning of the rope, and your soul's destiny is the rest of the rope into infinity and beyond.

If you stop and think about it, you will perform hundreds of thousands of activities to get ready to do something—big and small—in your lifetime. You get out of bed in the morning, put on some clothes, grab something to eat, brush your teeth, go to work, get ready for a meeting, wrap up your workday, drive home, have dinner, and relax with a TV show or movie. Those who are unmarried may go out on a date or see some friends, while those who are married and have children will tend to family duties.

Whether married or single, it's natural to think about the next big thing that will happen in your life—what it will take to be ready for the next job, the next promotion, the next move, or the next vacation. We've all been there, day in and day out.

That said, it always surprises me that so few of us think about what will happen in the afterlife. While I understand that the significance of preparing to meet the Creator of the Universe isn't something people often think about—or even want to consider—you should be aware that it's out there. Being ready to meet Jesus is off the Richter scale compared to anything else we're getting ready for—as well it should be.

I hope you *will* consider that day when you will meet Jesus, because your response will add an entirely different, positive perspective to how you live and the daily choices you make.

Perhaps one of the greatest stories of the last century that underscores the lack of preparation and long-term planning was the shocking catastrophe of the *RMS Titanic*, which sank on April 15, 1912.

When the *Titanic* was launched, the passenger ship was twice as long and more than half as wide as a football field and billed as the largest movable man-made object ever constructed. The *Titanic* was so colossal that "not even God could sink it," said newspaper reports. On its maiden voyage from Southampton, England, to New York City, the towering passenger liner carried 2,223 passengers and crew members.

The crew, however, had only done one lifeboat drill while the ship was docked before launch, but even if the crew had been better trained and each lifeboat had been loaded properly after the massive ship hit an iceberg, there was only sufficient space for about half of those onboard, or about 1,200 people.

The *Titanic* could carry sixty-four lifeboats but undertook its voyage with only twenty. Once the ship hit the iceberg, many of the launched lifeboats did not carry as many people as they could have. Thus, only 705 of the 2,223 passengers and crew survived the tragic sinking. (Talk about false confidence and hubris!)

Two thoughts come to mind regarding one of the biggest disasters in commercial maritime history.

- First, there was inadequate preparation for a potential disaster prior to launch.
- Second, the architects and builders believed that the *Titanic* was unsinkable when the reality was that the ship was quite capable of sinking. They failed to plan for this contingency.

What often gets overlooked is how the *Titanic*'s demise also represents an incredible study of how humans react when faced with inevitable and imminent death, which was the situation onboard the ship after striking an iceberg and taking on water. Think about this: How many of us will ever know that our lives will be snuffed out in two hours?

Virtually none of us. These days, sudden death strikes like a thunderbolt: car crashes, heart attacks, and airline disasters happen in a matter of seconds. At the other end of the spectrum, people rarely die quickly from contracting a disease, and modern medicine can extend life for months or years. **Notwithstanding those marvelous medical achievements, about two people die every second of every day somewhere in the world.**

Speaking for myself, one of the closest times I thought sudden death was imminent happened in my late thirties when I was flying home from a surf trip to Bali, Indonesia, in my late thirties. After the Garuda Airlines flight lifted off from Jakarta International Airport in Indonesia, we were at cruising altitude over the Pacific Ocean when the jet suddenly nose-dived.

My traveling comrades and I fell out of our seats (we had paid little attention to the seatbelt sign) and tumbled around the floor of the economy section. As the plane continued to free-fall, I was sure we were heading straight into the ocean.

Fortunately, the pilots regained control of the aircraft, and we pulled ourselves back into our seats and immediately buckled our seat belts. But I must confess that my first thought was not about Jesus and eternal life with Him. Sure, I acknowledged Him back then as God, but I'm not sure He was my No. 1 priority in life at the time, which would have been a shame *if* we were "going in," as they say.

So, imagine—if you can—what it must have been like standing on the upper deck of the *Titanic* after the last lifeboat had been lowered into the water. Soon, very soon, you know you will die a horrible death, either by drowning in the icy water or being crushed by a huge metal object breaking apart. Knowing you are standing on the precipice of eternity, would you fall to your knees and pray to the Lord of the Universe? Or would you look to the heavens, confused, angry, or bitter regarding what's about to happen?

For us, it's highly unlikely that we will know we will die at a particular moment or in a short period of time. But whether death is imminent or its timing unknown, it behooves us to be prepared for that day.

Because we only get one chance.

The story of the *Titanic* and Jesus' statements in Matthew 7 underscore the type of preparation that's necessary before we take our last breath here on Earth.

That preparation is not happening these days because the world is full of endless distractions to keep us from our real purpose and what's truly important for today and eternity. The world offers an endless script of things to do and accomplish before achieving a certain level of success, identity, and respect. We're constantly being told about the next best thing—the newest electronic device, the recent release of a streaming series or TV show, a new restaurant that's packed each evening . . . on and on it goes. The world focuses on meeting a temporal need or desire that keeps us busy with tantalizing, continuous consumption.

Tune out all that stuff. We were created in God's image, and all of us have a God-shaped vacuum in the shape of a heart longing to be filled with true meaning, authenticity, and purpose.

In C.S. Lewis's book, *The Screwtape Letters*, the master devil, known as Screwtape, counsels his young apprentice Wormwood about reliable techniques that lead souls away from God's truths. **It's the devil's business, explains Screwtape, to divert human**

minds from the present and the eternal by leading them into the past or the future, where anxiety and fear both live.

That's where we are today with the constant pursuit of wealth, status, and "stuff," but that chase guarantees you'll come up empty-handed and unfulfilled. Just look at the news or the supermarket tabloids. Ask yourself truthfully: Does it really look like the people who "have it all together" really have it all together? Unfortunately, too many people never realize this and allow far too much water to pass beneath the bridge of life, resulting in time that can never be recovered.

Time . . . it's like what a very wealthy and aging friend of mine said to me a few years ago: "I can buy anything I want, but I cannot buy more time." He spoke these words with an aroma of regret.

If you're a young adult or in your forties or even fifties, the passage of time likely isn't at the forefront of your thoughts, but perhaps today's turmoil has caused you to rethink whether the usual pursuits of life were worth it. Maybe you're among those who left their old jobs or were forced to take on different endeavors in recent years. Whatever your situation was, I'm willing to wager that once life got back to a "new normal" and your work situation stabilized, you probably fell back into the same old habits and ways of doing things.

Or perhaps you're feeling dissatisfied and wondering whether you have been doing things in your best interest in the short and long term. If you're thinking this way, it's time to consider this question: **If there is a God, how do I get ready to meet Him?**

This question could make all the difference for you.

For a moment, let me present you with a few glorious truths:

1. God is love, and all who live in love live in God, and God lives in them (1 John 4:16).
2. Jesus Christ is the same yesterday, today, and forever (Hebrews 13:8).

The wonderful news of Jesus Christ is that He lived the life we should live and died the death we should have. He is still here for us to cling to.

Because of the miracle of God's grace (also known as "God's riches at Christ's expense"), you can be set free not by what you do or who you are but by what you receive when you believe in Him.

Consider these two passages of Scripture:

> For it is by grace you have been saved, through faith—and this is not from yourselves, it is the gift of God—not by works, so that no one can boast.
>
> —EPHESIANS 2:8-9 (NIV)

> For God so loved the world that he gave his one and only Son, that whoever believes in him shall not perish but have eternal life. For God did not send His Son into the world to condemn the world, but to save the world through him.
>
> —JOHN 3:16-17 (NIV)

No personal effort is needed to receive this eternal security blanket; just a humble acknowledgment, a contrite heart, gracious acceptance, and wholehearted commitment. Then you can let the real purposeful living begin.

Are you ready to embrace these great truths that can take you on a new life trajectory? Are you ready to change how you've approached life up to this point?

Let me stop here and issue a warning: It will feel very uncomfortable to unpack and eliminate learned behavior. You must be willing to be stripped naked of all the presuppositions about how things should work and what is expected of you. You must be ready to be reduced to just "me" and allow Jesus to do His work in you and through you.

If you are willing, reconstruction can begin on the firmest foundation you could ever hope for. He will lead you to the point where you stop making excuses and just do what you know is right.

To be ready to meet your Creator requires a simple act of faith and a humble receipt of unfathomable and unmerited grace. It's not that complicated . . . just sometimes difficult to grasp, especially for the "overanalyzers" among us.

If you stop and think about it, life at the very end is a personal matter, regardless of how many loved ones are at your bedside. Job in the Old Testament said it best:

> "Naked I came from my mother's womb, and naked I will depart. The Lord gave and the Lord has taken away; may the name of the Lord be praised."
>
> —Job 1:21 (NIV)

Since every single one of us is born, lives for a period of time, and then dies, the question at the end will be: **"What did I live for?"**

I recall what happened after Catherine made it through those tough weeks in late 2008 and began her slow recovery in 2009. My dear friend and mentor, Sherm Harmer, asked me to teach a one-day course for his students in the Master of Real Estate Science program at the University of San Diego. Sherm had become my confidant and development consultant when I was seeking to build a large condominium project adjacent to the

Lafayette Hotel near downtown San Diego.

At the time, another friend told me that Sherm had a stellar business and personal reputation in San Diego development and political circles. Given the project's scope, we hired "The Sherminator," which turned out to be one of the best decisions of my life, even though the project never went forward after a fifteen-year effort. Sherm had my back and advised me through the various difficult chapters of the journey.

When I really wanted to pull the plug on the project, Sherm knew my greater desire was to pay everyone back—friends and others who had entrusted me with their investment money. I didn't want to file for bankruptcy, as many other developers did when the Great Recession hit, so I hung on at great financial and emotional expense and eventually returned everyone's money. Even though the effort took seventeen years, those were some of the sweetest checks I ever wrote.

At any rate, when Sherm asked me to speak to his students, he gave me a topic: "What to Do with a Real Estate Asset That Really Wants to Die But You Can't Let It." Sherm told me not only to advise the students on all the technical things we did and why I hung in there for years, but he also wanted me to discuss how I felt about the experience.

While preparing for the day-long course, I had to take some time to reflect on my values and what I considered important in a work situation, beyond just making money.

My parents had raised me to think first about doing a good job for whoever I worked for and realize that the money would follow. While that was not always the case in my forty-plus years of business experience, I knew this was an excellent way to approach business relationships—and the game of life.

One document I produced in the class handouts was the

following poem by Michael Josephson, a former attorney and founder of the Josephson Institute of Ethics in Los Angeles. I didn't think I could say it any better and still don't:

What Will Matter

Ready or not, someday it will all come to an end.
There will be no more sunrises, no minutes, no hours, or no days.
All the things you collected, whether treasured or forgotten, will pass to someone else.
Your wealth, fame, and temporal power will shrivel to irrelevance.
Your grudges, resentments, frustrations, and jealousies will finally disappear.
So too, your hopes, ambitions, plans, and to-do list will expire.
The wins and losses that once seemed so important will fade away.
It won't matter where you came from or what side of the tracks you lived on at the end.
It won't matter whether you were beautiful or brilliant.
Even your gender and your skin color will be irrelevant.
So, what will matter? How will the value of your days be measured?
What will matter is not what you bought but what you built,
Not what you got but what you gave.
What will matter is not your success but your significance.
What will matter is not what you learned but

what you taught.

What will matter is every act of integrity, compassion, courage, or sacrifice that enriched, empowered, or encouraged others to emulate your example.

What will matter is not your competence but your character.

What will matter is not how many people you knew but how many will feel a lasting loss when you are gone.

What will matter is not your memories but the memories that will live in those who loved you.

What will matter is how long you will be remembered, by whom and for what.

Living a life of meaning doesn't happen by accident.

It is not a matter of circumstances but of choices.

Choose to live a life that matters.

I will never forget the looks in some students' eyes when I read this poem and explained that "matters of the heart" should trump the almighty return on investment that is critical to every real estate transaction. As evidence, I shared that the final seventeen-year return on our investment in the Lafayette Hotel was not that great financially, but from the standpoint of the heart, it was off the charts.

This is one big reason why I urge you to live a life that makes the inevitable meeting with God and your eternity something to look forward to with great anticipation.

A classic Christmas movie our family watches every year is *Elf*, a holiday gem starring Will Ferrell. The main character is Buddy the Elf, a human raised by Santa's elves after being accidentally picked up at an orphanage by Santa one Christmas Eve thirty years earlier.

In the film, Buddy ventures out from the North Pole to find his birthfather since it's clear he's not like any of the other elves. While working at Gimbels Department Store in New York during Christmas, he becomes aware that there will be a "Santa" greeting little kids the next day.

Of course, this is not the "real" Santa like the Santa back at the North Pole, whom Buddy misses terribly. Without regard for who can hear him in Gimbel's, Buddy yells at the top of his lungs, "I know him! I know him!"[1]

His knowledge of Santa is a heart connection, not just a head connection. Would you feel comfortable standing before a large crowd and crying out, "I know Him! I know Him!"?

That's a rhetorical question, but I wanted to illustrate the importance of having an extravagant heart connection with Jesus. Let His words encourage you:

> "I tell you the truth, everyone who acknowledges me publicly here on earth, the Son of Man will also acknowledge in the presence of God's angels."
>
> —LUKE 12:8 (NLT)

Therefore, we need to be ready to tell others about our relationship with Jesus.

1 If you would like to watch this hilarious scene, go to YouTube and use these search words: Buddy the Elf, I know him!

When our youngest daughter, Georgiana, was around nine years old, Catherine organized a dozen young girls to come to our house once a month for food, fun, and biblical fellowship. My wife saw this as an opportunity to help Georgiana and her friends understand God's love for them, what it means to love God and others, and give them a firm foundation in Christ. This "God's Girls" crew would stay together all the way through high school.

One evening, Catherine prepared a list of questions for each girl to ask each other, questions like:

- "What is your favorite color?"
- "What is your favorite flower?"
- "What is your favorite food?"

She then paired up the girls. The twist was that the girl asking the questions would also have to give the answers for the girl she was asking. Well, the outcome was predictable. Very few guesses were accurate. When Catherine asked why that happened, the girls agreed they hadn't spent enough time together.

Isn't spending time together what a relationship is all about? When we spend time with Jesus and converse with Him, telling Him about the issues in our lives, a miraculous, inexplicable, and supernatural bond forms. You can be released to be all God intended you to be and love others as you know you are loved.

So, make a new friend this week. Call a family member or old friend and tell them you love them and care about them. Have someone over for dinner, do something kind for a stranger. Doing so sets the stage for the rest of your life on planet Earth. People will see the light within you, as Jesus said:

> "In the same way, let your good deeds shine out for all to see, so that everyone will praise your heavenly Father."
>
> —MATTHEW 5:16 (NLT)

Be sure to stay as close to Jesus as you can. When you yield to Him fully committed, an unaffected loveliness will flow, and the commonplace will become important. Sunsets will seem more magnificent. Even the smallest things will be enhanced in ways you could have never imagined. When you make Him No. 1 in your life, you can punch your ticket to eternal bliss and exponentially enhance your time on Earth.

Now, are you ready for a different approach?

3

Are You Ready to Be Ready?

"By failing to prepare, you are preparing to fail."

—Ben Franklin, one of the Founding Fathers

I understand my chapter title may seem redundant, but for some people, getting ready to perform any task, whether large or small, involves endless preparation. At some point, action needs to happen.

The phrase "paralysis by analysis" exists for a reason. Would you say that you're a deliberate person? Or are you the type who's addicted to the adrenaline rush of going for it, as in . . . shooting first and aiming second?

Notwithstanding my hardwiring for deliberate preparation, I did have moments of "shooting first and aiming second" as a younger man, like during my first trip to Hawaii in 1974, when my buddies and I came across a blowhole on Oahu. I was twenty-one, an avid surfer and college student. I told my friends I was taking a "gap year" to "improve my craft"—surfing, that is.

That day, several of us stood atop a rocky reef and—notwithstanding a calm ocean—watched a plume of ocean water shoot up through a blowhole, which is formed when sea caves grow landwards into a vertical shaft when seawater bursts through a gaping vent. While watching another fountain of water launch into the sky, one of my friends had a crazy idea: "Let's jump into the blowhole and see what happens."

To a bunch of testosterone-juiced young men, his idea made perfect sense, so much so that I volunteered to go first. (Yes, I was that stupid, and yes, this was definitely out of character—and not recommended from a water safety standpoint.)

I checked things out between chutes of water erupting like a geyser through the blowhole. When I peered into the blowhole and saw a pool of water that looked deep enough to jump into, I figured I was good to go.

When the next surge of water arrived, I leaped into the blowhole. The next thing I knew, I was sucked back into the ocean as the water receded. Somehow, I missed hitting rock that passed inches above my head.

Once I reached the open water, I was jacked by my exploit and heard my buddies' cheers. It might have been foolish to jump into the unknown like that, but I felt terrific about what I had done when it was over.

What about you? When was the last time you stretched yourself? It's good to extend ourselves sometimes (but not by jumping into blowholes), yet many of us struggle with wondering whether we're good enough to pull something off. While we don't have to know everything before jumping feet first, knowledge or experience gives us security and direction. Therein lies the dilemma: we know preparation is required, but unless we take the proverbial leap of faith and commit, we may miss the opportunity to experience something positive that could impact us for the rest of our lives.

Two dominating reasons why people do not act are their fear of failure or how they might look to others if they mess up. They are also afraid that the outcome may not be the one they would have liked.

Listen, I get it. Fear and anxiety live in everyone at some level, which is why we spend a lot of time making sure we're doing what we're supposed to do and making sure things are right with ourselves and the world around us before taking action. What we don't spend a lot of time doing is getting ready for what comes after our last breath is drawn. It's *that* preparation that can add immeasurable positive meaning to the time we have left on this earth.

Statistically, suppose a human being lives to eighty years of age. In that case, he or she will make some 770,000 decisions regarding readiness in their lifetime, according to a poll commissioned by the makers of the Puzzler Mind Gym 3D game.

The average person makes twenty-seven decisions per day or more than one per hour. Wouldn't now be a good time to decide that you need to be making plans on how you will spend eternity?

I like to joke that I was a Boy Scout coming out of the womb since I always look for something to organize and prepare for. I love to make plans, whether for a day trip to the beach, a shopping trip to the supermarket, getting approval for a development project, or researching an African safari. Jay is my name, and planning is my game.

I used to carry three good-sized baskets in the back of my SUV, which I'd fill with items everyone could use in emergencies or a natural disaster like an earthquake. My wife, Catherine, would good-naturedly tell friends that if anyone needs a winter coat, a black trash bag, an adjustable wrench, or a Band-Aid, just ask Jay when he pulls up. At some point, I realized three baskets were overkill. The number of baskets has since been reduced to two.

There is a certain comfort in being prepared, but one can also be *too* prepared, like when two of my five grandkids asked me to go skydiving with them to celebrate their eighteenth and twenty-first birthdays.

I couldn't say no, but I wanted to be prepared for what I was getting into, so I researched death rates for skydiving and spoke to several experienced skydivers. Notwithstanding the actual casualty percentages, I was tied up in knots emotionally and physically. People do die jumping out of an airplane! Maybe not often, but it happens.

I guess I wasn't as adventurous as I was in my occasional misguided days of youth. But I decided to go for it anyway since I didn't want to disappoint my grandchildren.

On the morning the small aircraft lifted into the air, I prayed for God's peace that passes all understanding so I would not pass out in fear as the tiny plane slowly climbed to a jumping-out attitude. As we leveled out and my instructor went through a checklist of last-minute preparations, I thought I was calm until the instructor told me to swing my legs over the edge of the tiny plane's open door at 12,000 feet.

Still, I didn't panic. I tried remembering what the instructor told me back on the ground—that I was more likely to die of a shark attack than perish in a tandem parachuting accident—but it wasn't helping!

Well, I jumped out and lived to talk about it—and made an awesome memory with two of my precious grandchildren. However, I *did not* follow up by bungee jumping over the Zambezi

River in Africa with my son-in-law, Scott Schreckengaust, and grandson, John. There are limits, right?

Which brings me to an important question: How should we best cope with anxiety and fear? One can practice "de-catastrophizing," a psychological approach to breaking down what the silly brain says *could* happen but usually doesn't—those "potential" worst-case scenarios that seek a place in our minds.

And we can also trust in God's Word:

> . . . do not be anxious about anything, but in everything by prayer and supplication with thanksgiving let your requests be made known to God. And the peace of God, which surpasses all understanding, will guard your hearts and your minds in Christ Jesus.
>
> —PHILIPPIANS 4:6-7 (ESV)

Isaiah 41:13 (ESV) reminds us of this:

> For I, the Lord your God,
> hold your right hand;
> it is I who say to you, "Fear not,
> I am the one who helps you."

It's comforting to know that when we invite Jesus to live in us, God Himself can be included in all our preparations, be they large or small.

And while the world is ready to provide advice on controlling anxiety and dealing with fear, one needs to consider whether there's an essential element missing from the world's approach to making potentially life-altering decisions without the end in view.

By the end, I mean the ultimate end . . . death on planet Earth and off into eternity. Not that risky human endeavors don't cause us to contemplate the risk of death, but we shouldn't have to stand over a blowhole, drop into a hundred-foot wave, or be tethered to a parachute instructor to realize that we should think about what lies beyond.

But here's the deal: the last thing the world wants us to do is keep us from focusing on what happens when we leave the planet. The world around us is designed to keep us off balance, insecure, and continually questioning what we need from one moment to the next for worldly happiness.

That's a shame because Jesus, through His Word, gives us many wonderful promises about how He sees us and how He longs to be included in our journey, no matter what we're dealing with in this life. Consider this:

> "For I know the plans I have for you," declares the Lord, "plans to prosper you and not to harm you, to give you a future and a hope. Then you will call on me and come and pray to me, and I will listen to you. You will seek me and find me when you seek me with all of your heart."
>
> —Jeremiah 29:11-14 (NIV)

We will find the proper preparation when we align ourselves with Jesus' words:

> "For which of you, desiring to build a tower, does not sit down first and count the cost, whether he has enough to complete it?"
>
> —Luke 14:28 (ESV)

Jesus approves of adequate and thoughtful preparation in everything we do. What we might consider a small matter could be huge in His plans for our lives and for the impact on the lives of others.

Worldly success often overlooks the fact that whether we win or lose, succeed or fail, we can accept ourselves because we are followers of Jesus and know who we are and Whose we are.

Our identity is in Him. Our righteousness, our "right-ness," is in Him.

In John 16:13 (NIV), Jesus says:

> "But when he, the Spirit of truth, comes, he will guide you into all the truth. He will not speak on his own; he will speak only what he hears, and he will tell you what is yet to come."

When we claim Jesus as our Lord and Savior, He resides in us forever. We just need to give him room to be the Good Shepherd:

> "My sheep hear my voice, and I know them, and they follow Me. I give them eternal life, and they shall never perish, and no one will snatch them out of my hand."
>
> —John 10: 27-28 (ESV)

What could be better than to be guided by God's Spirit and be eternally safe in His powerful hands?

The critical factor in being ready for anything, from a job interview to climbing Mount Everest, is this: everything needs to be in proper alignment with Jesus. When you're correctly calibrated with Him, you'll travel in the right direction and get to where He wants you to be. Remember, He will train and prepare you:

> I will instruct you and teach you in the way
> you should go;
> I will counsel you with my loving eye on you.
>
> —Psalm 32:8 (ESV)

When you submit daily to Jesus and express gratitude for what He did on the Cross, you're lined up to live life to the fullest for Him.

So where do good planning and preparation intersect with a careful and thoughtful reliance on Christ? The answer can be summed up in this verse from Scripture:

> So whether you eat or drink or whatever you do, do it all to the glory of God.
>
> —1 Corinthians 10:31 (NIV)

Now that's what I call living life to the fullest!

When I went skiing with a friend in Utah many years ago, strapping on skis for the first time, my friend told me we were taking the chairlift to the top and skiing down from there. I have to say that my youthful enthusiasm and perhaps a false sense of bravado got the better of me. I should've gone straight to the bunny slopes and taken a lesson or had someone show me how to ski. After all, I had never tried the winter sport before.

But my friend was insistent, saying I could do it, so I followed him to the main chairlift, struggling to stay upright on my skis. When we got to the top of the mountain, I crashed just getting off the lift! Once I righted myself, I shuffled over to the precipice of the run. When I peered over the edge, I saw a white, bumpy slope that was very, very long and very, very steep.

"What do I do next?" I asked my friend.

He looked at me with a grin. "Just point the boards down the hill, and off you go."

I was such a fool. I did exactly what my friend told me to

do, and I fell in a heap every time I attempted to make a turn. I learned the hard way that I should have prepared myself to become a skier by starting on the bunny slopes, where I could have learned the basics of how to make a turn. That would have been the wiser path.

Don't too many of us go through life riding a lift to the mountaintop without being adequately prepared for the arrival? I'm afraid so. I would suggest that most of the time it's good to think about where you're going to end up before you embark on your journey . . . which has a spiritual application, of course. How much thought have you given to what will happen when you reach the mountaintop, so to speak, and Jesus is waiting for you?

When you're properly aligned with Jesus, you will see the world through His eyes. You will see who you are with the confidence that comes from knowing who He is because you brought Him into your life. Keep this thought in mind:

> Commit your works to the Lord,
> And your thoughts will be established.
>
> —PROVERBS 16:3 (NKJV)

What could be better than committing your works to the Lord and becoming all you were designed to be?

One of the beautiful aspects of Christianity is that you're invited to the ultimate "come as you are" party. No need for costumes or makeup or endless years of striving for suitability in God's presence.

So don't worry about what others will think about you. The sooner you realize that, the sooner you will grow in ways you didn't know were possible.

Be encouraged and take a deep breath. Say this out loud:

I will first find out what I need from my Creator, and then I will take intelligent steps to move forward with joy and without regard to the outcome.

I'm not saying there's a formula for this, but if there were, it would go like this: You plus Jesus equals perfect planning and preparation, even if the outcome isn't what you expected or desired. But facing unexpected results builds fortitude, humility, and resiliency, so relax and leave the outcome up to Him. Remember, *you are enough . . . and you will always be enough with Jesus in you.*

This week, choose something new to do that stretches you out of your comfort zone. I'm not saying you must jump out of an airplane but be sure to appropriately plan what you're going to do and then go for it. He will meet you where you are! Spread your wings because you are alive. The gift of life is an amazing adventure.

I'll close this chapter with a speech from the 26th president of the United States, Theodore Roosevelt. I've kept a copy alongside my other important papers because I consider these thoughts from Teddy Roosevelt important enough to reflect upon occasionally.

The Man in the Arena

It is not the critic who counts; not the man who points out how the strong man stumbles, or where the doer of deeds could have done better.

The credit belongs to the man who is actually in the arena, whose face is marred by dust and sweat and blood; who strives valiantly; who errs, who comes up short again and again, because there is no effort

> without error and shortcoming; but who actually strives to do the deeds; who knows great enthusiasm, the great devotions; who spends himself in a worthy cause; who at the best knows in the end the triumph of high achievement, and who at worst, if he fails, at least fails while daring greatly, so that his place will never be with those cold and timid souls who know neither victory or defeat.

Are you willing to step into the arena and put yourself out there?

I hope you are because that's all part of getting ready to meet the Lord one day.

4

Are You Ready to See Yourself as Jesus Sees You?

You know the day destroys the night
Night divides the day
Tried to run, tried to hide
Break on through to the other side

—lyrics from the Doors' song,
Break on Through (To the Other Side)

I was born into a middle-class upbringing, the son of a traveling salesman and a homemaker living in Charlotte, North Carolina. Even though I didn't have a silver spoon childhood, I received something better: my parents gave me and my three siblings a stable and loving faith-based home, although Dad and Mom both had issues with alcohol.

I remember my mother as the nurturing type who liked to write when she had extra time by penning plays for the school, articles for the PTA newsletter, or an occasional magazine submission. Dad, however, was often gone most of the week because he sold eyewear on the road and had accounts to call on.

When I was three, we moved across the country to the Los Angeles area, first settling in a leafy Pasadena neighborhood. Nine years later, when I was twelve, we moved a short distance to Sierra Madre, where my parents found a nice home at the base of the San Gabriel Mountains.

This was the 1960s, a time when the chaparral-covered foothills were hidden behind a thick haze of smog for most of the year. The brown polluted air from millions of exhaust-belching cars and trucks clogging the roads stung our eyes and choked our lungs because the San Gabriel Valley—known as the "Valley of Smoke"—sat in a basin.

We were a devout Catholic family that attended Mass every Sunday and ate tuna fish casserole topped with cornflakes on Friday nights. I attended St. Rita's Catholic School in Sierra Madre, where the Augustinian nuns ruled with an iron fist. Fortunately for my situation, the nuns liked me because I listened in class, did what I was told, and followed the rules. I was voted president of every class through eighth grade and was an altar boy who didn't make waves. In the spirit of full confession, though, I did eat some unconsecrated hosts in the vestibule area before the 6:30 a.m. Mass on a few occasions to stave off hunger pangs.

Meanwhile, the dirty air took its toll. Because of increasing respiratory issues with my siblings and me, we moved to the surf town of San Clemente in 1968, located halfway between San Diego and Los Angeles. San Clemente's most famous part-time resident was President Richard Nixon, whose sprawling beachfront mansion was called "The Western White House" by the media.

My parents enrolled me in San Clemente High in the middle of my sophomore year. Once again, I excelled academically and was voted junior class president and student body president

Have van, will travel. I was quite the surf hobo in my younger days, a time when the Beach Boys' "Surfing Safari" could have been the theme song for adventures that took me from top surfing spots in California to secluded surf breaks in Baja and Mainland Mexico, Hawaii, the South Pacific, and Indonesia.

for my senior year. I was an alternate to the Boys State organization[1] and spoke to local fraternal organizations about youth in America. I helped stop an unpopular airport from becoming a reality in Orange County. I participated in philanthropic endeavors while still earning superior grades on my report card. On top of all that, I held down various part-time jobs to earn gas and dating money.

Upon graduation, I was awarded a partial scholarship to Georgetown University in Washington, DC, where I had an eye on earning a law degree and perhaps getting into politics. I dreamed of winning an election to the US House of Representatives one day.

Here's why I'm relaying all of this background info: even though I got off to a great start in life—doing well in school, winning ASB elections, earning a law degree, branching out into real estate, and marrying well with Catherine—I had an annoying sense that I wasn't good enough.

I'm unsure where this feeling came from. My parents set reasonable expectations for me, but I created a high bar for myself and what I wanted to do with my life. An uneasy feeling that I wasn't good enough would linger for many years into adulthood and my marriage.

My journey toward meaningful self-acceptance didn't seriously begin until I was in my late thirties and newly married to Catherine. We were living in San Diego, and a friend of mine invited me to a theatrical production at his church in Rancho Peñasquitos. His congregation was hosting an evangelistic drama called *Heaven's Gates and Hell's Fury* that asked a fundamental question: *What will happen to you when you die?*

---

1 Boys State was a participatory program in which students become part of the operation of local, county, and state government. Boys State was founded in 1935 by the American Legion to counter the socialism-inspired Young Pioneer Camps. Girls State was formed in 1937. These days, the organization is coed and known as Boys/Girls State.

The cast was made up of people from the church who were taught to dramatize the reality of what happens to all of us immediately after death. The Bible teaches that there is a Book of Life containing the names of everyone who has accepted Jesus as their Lord and Savior. If your name is in the Book of Life, you get to enter heaven. If it isn't, then it's off to eternal separation from God. (Yikes!)

There were nearly a dozen skits to demonstrate this premise, but the one that hit me between the solar plexus was about two young parents who dropped their kids off at youth group one night and ate dinner at a nearby restaurant. When they returned to pick up their kids, their youngsters were excited to tell them they had heard the gospel, accepted Jesus into their hearts, and become Christians. The parents were only mildly interested. As the children gabbed about the exciting evening, everything changed in an instant when—boom! A truck T-boned the minivan, killing all four instantly.

The scene shifted to a heavenly setting, with an angel standing behind a podium, the Book of Life open. That's when the parents learned their names were not in the Book of Life, but the kids' names were. You can guess who was welcomed into heaven and who was banished to eternal punishment and damnation in a very horrific, theatrical way.

After the drama skits, the pastor made a traditional altar call. I was so taken by what I heard and saw that evening that I was scared to death. I sure didn't want to end up in hell, permanently separated from God, so I had a decision to make: Did I believe that God so loved the world that He gave His one and only Son so that everyone who believes in Him will not perish but have eternal life (John 3:16)? Or did I not?

The answer that night was an all-the-way yes. I had always

believed in God, but this feeling was different. It wasn't just about knowing. It was about owning what I already knew at a much deeper level. Sensing I was at a crossroads, I decided to go forward.

It turned out to be an eerie situation: one moment, I was sitting near the back of the auditorium, and the next, I found myself at the front of the church, where someone explained the gospel to me again and led me in a prayer to receive Jesus Christ into my heart.

I still don't know how I got from my seat to the stage. It was as if I were somehow transported without my feet moving. Looking back on this experience, I would like to say that I was saved by fear but sustained by love because "the fear of the Lord is the beginning of wisdom, and knowledge of the Holy One is understanding" (Proverbs 9:10, ESV).

So, you would think, after hearing my story about what happened in my late thirties, that my life became a stroll down a primrose path, that I had everything figured out. You'd think I'd finally accepted myself for who I was since Christianity teaches that all who trust in Jesus are loved and forgiven by God, regardless of their flaws.

But that didn't happen.

I still struggled with feelings of worthlessness and self-doubt and was filled with negative thoughts, the classic symptoms of low self-esteem that can harm our physical and mental health and our relationships with others and with God. I was not alone in how I viewed myself: several studies indicate that 85 percent of Americans suffer from low self-esteem, meaning we go through bouts of low self-worth or have our confidence shaken from time to time.

Low self-esteem was amplified by a little voice in my head that constantly criticized me, causing me to doubt my God-given abilities or judgment. Sometimes, a lack of faith in myself prevented me from taking calculated risks to better myself, setting ambitious goals, and acting on them.

And this admission may surprise you: I kept hearing my inner critic even after I recommited my life to Christ as an adult.

The world's pushdown that I didn't measure up somehow was relentless since I had a new enemy—Satan. I know Satan is a scary word, but he is a real-world problem, and he is out to deceive us. The Bible calls him the father of lies (John 8:44), which is interesting because the word *lie* means "a falsehood with the intent to deceive."

The world tells us that life is all about us—me, myself, and I—and that living beyond our means won't hurt us, or that there isn't any absolute truth—that truth is relative. We're told that a good job and having enough money in the bank will provide the happiness we need. We hear that we can watch over-sexed and violent movies and not be negatively impacted by them.

Which is total balderdash, of course.

It wasn't until I really devoted myself to studying the Bible, searching Scripture, and feeling the true weight of His biblical promises that I began to feel more comfortable in my skin and more self-accepting of who I was in Christ. I was blown away by what I was reading. Here are several biblical verses that helped me gain some much-needed perspective:

> As far as the east is from the west, so far does he remove our transgressions from us.
>
> — Psalm 103:12 (ESV)

> Therefore, if anyone is in Christ, he is a new creation. The old has passed away. Behold, the new has come.
>
> —2 CORINTHIANS 5:17 (ESV)

> There is no fear in love, but perfect love casts out all fear. For fear has to do with punishment, and whoever fears has not been perfected in love. We love him because he first loved us.
>
> —1 JOHN 4:18-19 (ESV)

> There is now therefore no condemnation for those who are in Christ Jesus.
>
> – ROMANS 8:1-2 (ESV)

I knew the Lord of the Universe, but even better, He knew me. Whenever I worried or was fearful, all I needed to do was remember God's promises that I was eternally forgiven, that He was with me and walked with me every minute of every day. He would give me daily direction and be there the moment I stepped over the other side into eternity. Jesus Himself said:

> "I give them eternal life, and they will never perish. No one can snatch them away from me . . ."
>
> —JOHN 10:28 (NLT)

Imagine Jesus saying that anyone who believes in Him will never die, and no one can take that individual away from Him!

Furthermore, why should I or any of us feel inferior when we have all that going for us?

We shouldn't . . . period.

I'll never forget when our youngest daughter, Georgiana (aka Gigi in our family), was about to enter high school, and Catherine sat her down one summer day for a mom-and-daughter talk. My wife knew all too well that our daughter lacked social awareness due to her autism, so to help Gigi, Catherine explained that high school girls could be socially rough, meaning they were catty and spiteful to those not in their cliques.

I loved hearing Gigi's response: "That's okay, Mom. I'm popular with God. I'm also popular with my family. And if I don't have any friends, then I'll always have my books."

Although at times over the years, Gigi's "Why me's?" about her condition were drenched in tears, she has always believed she is "fearfully and wonderfully made" (Psalm 139:14) and that God has a purpose for her life. God has revealed much to me through Gigi.

Once we have surrendered to Jesus and have given Him back the control He deserves, we realize God's view of us *never* changes. Our feelings about our distance from God based on our day-to-day performance may change, but His feelings do not. We *must* remember that thought and see ourselves as God sees us. When we do that, we produce monumental positive changes in our lives.

The world can offer some constructive pathways for improvement, but they are inherently limited without Jesus as part of the equation. For instance, I listened to a podcast by a famous actor and successful businessman about helping people understand how to address their problems, organize their lives, and lead successful lives. I appreciated that his ideas weren't about making a ton of money or filling their homes with stuff as a solution.

When I listened to this podcast, I was impressed with the solid steps he laid out for people. But one thing was missing—the spiritual side to life. Even if you followed his script to a tee, there's no getting around the fact that living without Jesus is like a donut: there's a hole in the middle of your heart.

How can any of us have real, permanent, and transformative hope for the future if this life is all there is? Because life can seem like a cruel joke, even in the best of times. Jesus is the next-level hope that transcends the inevitable highs and lows of our journey on planet Earth. Absolute *joy* comes from a consistent and obedient relationship with Jesus, who said this to His disciples:

> "I have told you these things so that you will be filled with my joy. Yes, your joy will flow!"
>
> – John 15:11 (NLT)

When life's going well, we feel elated. When hardships fall upon us, we may tend to sink into a rabbit hole of depression. The true joy available to believers in John 15:11 transcends the rolling waves of circumstance. You will find joyfulness when you have a constant in your life—a consistent relationship with Jesus. The joy of walking with the Lord daily will keep you levelheaded, no matter how high or low your circumstances are.

I saw that joy in a dear neighbor of ours. Her name was Harriett Booth, and we got to know her when she was in her early nineties. She was the spitting image of Gloria Stuart, the actress who played the elderly Rose Dawson Calvert in the celebrated movie *Titanic.*[2] In the early days of commercial airlines, Harriet was one of the first stewardesses—as flight attendants were called back then. She was also a pilot who

---

2 At the end of the movie, Rose dropped a diamond necklace with a blue diamond, known as "The Heart of the Ocean," into the Atlantic Ocean over the wreck site. The necklace was given to Rose by her then fiancé Cal Hockley (Billy Zane). She survived the Titanic's sinking and Cal did not.

became a Powder Puff champion after winning a cross-country air derby. While raising a family, she took her kids to school on horseback. Imagine doing that today.

Catherine and I loved dropping in to say hello to her and being regaled with stories from her fascinating life. The perpetual smile on her face reflected the ebullience of a woman who knew her days were coming to an end, yet had Jesus in her heart, which brought her great joy.

As Harriett neared her 101st birthday, we visited and paged through some of her many scrapbooks with her. Catherine and I asked Harriett what guiding and overarching principle she adhered to throughout her long life.

"Acceptance," she quickly replied. "Acceptance that I don't control what comes at me, but I control my response."

Her response resonated with Catherine and me because she reminded us that God loves us and accepts us just as we are, no matter what we have done, what we have been through, or will go through. He does not require us to be perfect to be accepted by Him.

The Bible teaches us that God's love is based on His grace, not on our merits or what we can do for Him. When we receive His grace, we can live more freely and without the baggage of low self-esteem.

This is how God views us when we place our trust in His Son:

> "I tell you, in the same way there will be more joy in heaven over one sinner who repents than over ninety-nine righteous people who have no need of repentance."
>
> —LUKE 15:7 (AMP)

Julius Charles Hare, a 19th-century English theological writer, once wrote:

> Be what you are. This is the first step to becoming better than you are.

Being viewed as perfect in His eyes every day—as you do your level best—is an awesome thought. How much more true richness awaits you?

Which leads me to these questions:

- Do you accept who you are?
- Do you see yourself as Jesus sees you?

God's undeniable affirmation of who you are and your inherent worth goes back to our very creation. In Genesis 1:26 (NIV), God said:

> "Let us make mankind in our image, in our likeness."

Every human being bleeds the same blood. All of our hearts push blood through our arteries and veins. We are all made up of the same proportions of minerals and liquids. Humans are the only creatures on Earth created in God's image. That also means we have a spiritual nature, which gives us the capacity to know God and have a relationship with Him. How cool is that?

Few things have filled me with more joy than graduating from the school of self-degradation and self-doubt into the ecstasy of self-acceptance through Jesus Christ. You can experience that same joy when you see yourself as Jesus sees you—as one of His precious children—and accept Him into your heart as you accept yourself. 1 John 3:1 (NLT) teaches us this:

> See how very much our Father loves us, for he calls us his children, and that is what we are! But the people who belong to this world don't recognize that we are God's children because they don't know him.

There's no reason to "belong to this world." You'll never see yourself as Jesus sees you if you do, so let these words from God fill you with confidence that you are His:

> "I have loved you, my people, with an
> everlasting love.
> With unfailing love I have drawn you to myself."
>
> —JEREMIAH 31:3 (NLT)

> . . . because you are precious to me.
> You are honored, and I love you.
>
> —ISAIAH 43:4 (NLT)

Don't let any self-doubts or ongoing mistakes rob you one iota of the righteousness and whiteness of the robes that enclose you as a follower of Jesus.

When your faith finally allows you to break through the wall of performance-based religion and into the throne room of Grace because of His love and sacrifice, you will never, ever be the same, nor will you ever want to be the same.

When that happens, you will be the most amazed person in the world. Your new sense of self will give you the desire to live your best life for God and others and will allow you to cut through the world's clutter with extraordinary grace and ease.

Sure, the storms of life will still hit, but He will always love you the same. Sure, there will be days when you are ashamed of your actions and the mistakes you made. He will still love you just the same. Even when you question everything, He will always love you the same.

The world will continue to look for opportunities to put you down, but the only thing that matters is whether Jesus Christ is your Lord and Savior. When you release any lingering self-doubts, you'll be ready to make the improvements God designed for you before time began.

Self-acceptance based on how Jesus sees you and not the way the world views you is a stepping stone toward an eternal existence that none of us can imagine, as Scripture reminds us:

> But as it is written,
> "What eye has not seen, nor ear heard,
> nor the heart of man imagine,
> what God has prepared for those who love Him."
>
> —1 CORINTHIANS 2:9 (ESV)

This week . . . be encouraged! Let God fill the hole in your heart as He has filled mine. Remember, He sees us as one of His own, a full heir of everything that belongs to Him (Galatians 4:7), which is why every blessing and every benefit that He promises—and all of Him—are available to us.

5

Are You Ready for True Friendship?

"Friendship is born at that moment when one person says to another, 'What! You too? I thought I was the only one.'"

—C. S. Lewis, British author and Christian thinker best known for *The Chronicles of Narnia* and *Mere Christianity*

I'll start with a series of questions:

- What is real friendship?
- What has become of real friendship in recent years?
- What is the world's approach to friendship?
- What is Jesus' approach to friendship?

An overarching principle I live by is that it's impossible to be consistently friendly to others unless you're friendly to yourself, which I define as giving yourself grace and being quick to forgive yourself for past mistakes. More on that to follow.

The world has messed up what real friendship should be, but if one takes the time, one can discover what meaningful friendships entail.

The American Psychological Association defines friendship as a "voluntary relationship between two or more people that is relatable and long-lasting and in which those involved tend to be concerned with meeting the others' needs and interests as well as satisfying their own desires." Friendships frequently develop through shared experiences that are mutually gratifying to both parties.

These days, signs of friendship include engaging in meaningful conversations and being accepting, honest, and dependable. Friends write encouraging texts, exercise and do physical activities together, exchange gifts and notes of affirmation, and willingly engage in tech-free dining. Friends love to hang out, watch big sporting events together, and eat yummy foods. No matter the culture or country you grew up in, friendships are important relationships throughout a person's lifespan.

Unfortunately, real friendship appears to be failing in great numbers and falling prey to technology-based relationships that mimic none of the attributes I've just described. In a word, I sense many people are lonely today.

Loneliness is a signal that something is wrong. According to a recent CNN article, one in four people is very lonely, with the majority of those people being young. I believe there's been an enormous increase in loneliness over the last twenty years, driven by the introduction of smartphones and social media.

I call it "head down" time—people preferring to engage their screens and tap and swipe rather than looking a friend or acquaintance in the eye at a coffee shop and partaking in give-and-take conversation and an honest exchange of ideas. The Covid-19 pandemic, without a doubt, exacerbated the lack of social connection and continues to be felt just about everywhere—in our personal interactions, in our schools, in our workplaces, and in our civic organizations.

It's a shame that so many of us have problems making friends because we're hard-wired for relationships with other humans. Those without robust social connections are less likely to live long, healthy lives filled with happiness. Mental health takes a hit too.

Conversely, true friendship is like true love: it's an outward-facing emotion that accepts and loves those we know well, despite our differences or the difficulties we encounter. It's based on a foundation of mutual trust, respect, and understanding. True friends are around each other and willing to share their thoughts and feelings openly. They value your opinions and boundaries and accept you for who you are. That's the way true friendship should work.

Friendships can be tricky. We all want to be known so we can be loved, but we also fear exposing our real selves.

Jesus threaded that needle and resolved and reconciled that tension when He gave His life for us. He both knows and accepts us to the depths of our sinfulness, and He loves us to infinity and beyond. When we realize this great truth, we have nothing to hide from Him or others. We are free to be ourselves.

The world's view of friendship is often a calculus that many go through when interacting with another individual: *If I continue to get to know this person, what's in it for me?*

This age-old question stems from the old saying, "You scratch my back, and I'll scratch yours," a concept that dates back to Roman times when the Latin phrase *quid pro quo* meant "something for something." In other words, when you ask for a favor, you know you'll be asked to do something for the other person sometime down the road.

Meaningful interaction with others is not about using a new friendship for your personal gain. People can smell an agenda from one hundred paces, so if you strike up a loaded conversation with someone you barely know to develop some sort of relationship that lines your pockets, you'll burn a bridge and never build a meaningful relationship with that person.

It's much better to go through life putting other people's interests and well-being before your own. Even better is treating others the way you want to be treated, as Jesus said in Luke 6:31 (NASB).

The traditional translation of this verse—"Do unto others as you would have them do unto you"—has long been known as the "Golden Rule." It's the gold standard for interpersonal relationships and is communicated in easy-to-understand words.

The Golden Rule of friendship states that if we want people to like us, then we need to make them feel loved and accepted. By making others feel good, they will want to be around us more. And if they are around us more, we can shine the light of Christ in their lives.

But as I look at the world around me, it's amazing how many people conveniently forget the Golden Rule, especially Monday through Saturday. It's as if Jesus' words travel through one ear and out the other on Sunday, even for many of the faithful.

Jesus said something else that has always stuck with me:

> "There is no greater love than to lay down one's life for one's friends."
>
> —John 15:13 (NLT)

Jesus was telling His disciples that there was no greater love than to give up the things they wanted to do and give of themselves to others. While very few of us will be asked to make the ultimate sacrifice and literally lay down our lives for a friend—like on the battlefield—we can still live with an attitude of living for others.

My good friend Dieter showed how he prioritizes others while on his way home one afternoon to Coronado, a charming town across the bay from downtown San Diego. As part of his weekday commute, he hops on the five-lane Coronado Bridge, which has a total length of 2.1 miles and rises to a height of 240 feet. Unfortunately, the picturesque span has become a magnet for desperate people wishing to end their lives by jumping into San Diego Bay, much like how people leap to their deaths from the Golden Gate Bridge in San Francisco.

As Dieter approached the top of the Coronado Bridge late one afternoon, a car suddenly stopped, blocking his lane. Quickly, a woman left her car and hustled over to the bridge's thirty-four-inch concrete sidewall. Bridge officials had installed four-inch-tall metal bird spikes on top of the low wall to deter would-be jumpers, which gave this woman pause.

The presence of the bird spikes prompted the woman, in her late thirties, to assess what she would do next. Dieter didn't hesitate. He quickly stopped, bolted from his car, and ran to the woman, yelling, "Don't!"

The Coronado Bridge's most distinctive element is its graceful S-curve across the azure-blue San Diego Bay, connecting downtown San Diego with the charming, upscale seaside community of Coronado. Unfortunately, the bridge has a tragic history of suicides and attempts in California, second only to the Golden Gate Bridge in San Francisco.

She looked up—in time to save her life. When he approached her, Dieter spoke to the woman lovingly and peacefully, reminding her that she had much to live for and that she had family and friends who loved her. The woman's countenance changed. She stood down until the police arrived.

Dieter didn't have to get involved, but he did. Similarly, I have a personal story of how someone else's selfless caring benefited me in a significant way. It happened when I flew with two friends in a small private plane from San Diego to Guerrero Negro, near a great surf spot halfway down the Baja California peninsula. We had packed our boards into the Piper Turbo and looked forward to dropping into some pristine barrels on the Mexican coastline.

On the way down, my pilot friend, Kelly, thought it would be fun to detour and spend the night in Mulejé on the Sea of Cortez, so we headed east. Kelly said Mulejé was a beautiful little spot with lush palm groves and swathes of green in an otherwise arid land.

Sounded like a nice diversion to me.

After flying for a half hour in an easterly direction, we noticed the sun was setting faster than we expected. *No bueno*. The dirt landing strip wouldn't be lit. We couldn't land in the dark.

But could we make it back to Guerrero Negro before we ran out of daylight? Their dirt strip wasn't lit either.

Sweaty palms time. Now we were in a race to see if we could land before total darkness enshrouded the landing strip. It looked like we had enough daylight, but we would be cutting it close.

As we made our approach to Guerrero Negro, the sun had long set. Just a hint of dusk remained. We circled the town in search of the landing strip. This was getting very serious.

Suddenly, in the gathering darkness, we saw a pair of light beams blinking at the end of what looked to be the runway.

"I'm going in," Kelly said. I'll admit that I whispered a prayer or two.

Kelly took aim and dropped the Piper Turbo in for a three-point landing. Boy, did it feel good to be on *terra firma* again.

After we taxied to a stop, the "lights" at the end of the runway moved. Turned out to be a truck driven by a local. He drove up as Kelly cut the engine. We all knew a little Spanish, and what we figured out—with a combination of our broken Spanish and the local's hand gestures—is that this hospitable *senõr* heard us circling the town and knew we were looking for the airstrip. He took it upon himself to park his *camíon* at the end of the runway with his headlights on. His selfless act saved our lives.

Looking back at this life-saving event, I realize that this simple act of caring was done by someone who heard the faint sound of an airplane propeller in the nearly nighttime sky and took the time to act.

We thanked him profusely. Looking back and reflecting on how quick our post-landing interaction was, I wish we had insisted on taking this hombre to a nearby cantina and sharing a pitcher of *cerveza*!

But I was reminded: How many of us take the time to really listen or watch for an opportunity to assist someone else in need?

As we swim through life, there is an undercurrent in our societal waters promoting disparagement, disunity, disharmony, and distance from one another at an accelerating pace.

We need to put our phones down and step away from the computer.

We need to ask ourselves whether our lives are defined by the likes we receive on Facebook, Instagram, or TikTok reels.

We need to ask ourselves if we have recently or ever extended ourselves for anyone's benefit without the expectation of a return . . . gone the extra mile. As Jesus said:

> "If a soldier demanded that you carry his gear for a mile, carry it two miles. Give to those who ask, and don't turn away from those who want to borrow."
>
> —Matthew 5:41-42 (NLT)

I wonder how many young people with hundreds or thousands of "friends" on social media have real flesh-and-blood friends. I fear they are empty vessels craving what they cannot get because they won't let go of what the world defines as "fulfilling."

We cannot receive what will truly and meaningfully fill us until we are willing to risk losing everything we think matters.

Real friends seek avenues of reconciliation. Real friends feel the depth of something they may not want to face, but they realize that true friendship and caring for others are inextricably linked to being able to forgive themselves and others.

In Matthew 6:14-15 (NLT), Jesus said:

> "If you forgive those who sin against you, your heavenly Father will forgive you. But if you refuse to forgive others, your Father will not forgive your sins."

Apparently, the ability to forgive others (and ourselves) is a deeply important concept that Jesus strongly emphasized during his time on Earth. Think about it: God completely and eternally forgives us of our sins, and then the times we wrong others, we're to do the same for those around us.

It's good to remember that Jesus died for our sins and for the sins of those who wronged us. What we need today is *wild* and *unrestrained* forgiveness. If you're sideways with someone, whether it be your spouse, your child, your co-worker, or your friend, turn to the Lord in prayer and be reminded of the sacrifice that He made for you and was made for the person who wronged you or whom you may have wronged. If you are struggling to forgive someone, seek the Lord in prayer and ask Him to help you understand the other person's feelings. Ask God to reveal your role and any wrongdoing. Pray for patience too.

As a society, we are on the wrong track on this issue and must backtrack to a better way and a better day.

At the height of my "busy career" some years ago, I stopped to fill my gas tank before heading into downtown San Diego on my morning commute. Before my tank was full, a woman pulled in behind me to also fill her tank. When she stepped out of the car, I noticed she was crying. I didn't stop to ask if I could help—probably because I was "too busy" thinking about my first meeting of the morning. Looking back on this event, I must confess that I will remember that failure for the rest of my life. I could have been a friendly face to her when she felt like some part of her world was coming undone at that moment.

What happened that day reminds me of an old saying: **"Everyone wants to save the world, but no one wants to help Mom do the dishes."**

Look for opportunities to display friendship. What we see depends on what we are looking for.

Finally, what is Jesus's approach to friendship? Consider these words:

> "No longer do I call you servants, for the servant does not know what his master is doing; but I have called you friends, for all that I have heard from my Father I have made known to you."
>
> —John 15:15 (ESV)

There is tremendous spiritual power in friendship.

For the unfathomable gift of eternal life, Jesus was at the opposite eternal end of the *quid pro quo* mantra. This is reflected by His desire to fulfill His destiny and give His everything so we could be free. Our response should simply be to receive, to believe, and to commit.

Acting friendly may not always produce immediate results,

but we can leave situations with the handprints and footprints of Jesus and remember the words from Ecclesiastes 3:2 (NLT):

> A time to be born and a time to die.
> A time to plant and a time to harvest

We are merely seed sowers; God controls the outcome.

The apostle Paul reminds us to "put off the old self, which belongs to your former manner of life and is corrupt through deceitful desires, and to be renewed by the spirit of your minds, and to put on the new self, created after the likeness of God in true righteousness and holiness" (Ephesians 4:22-24, ESV).

Only true friendship will change your life permanently, first with Jesus, then with yourself and others. That is the one true cosmic sequencing. Once you are assured that Jesus is your friend, you can—without restraint—be a true friend to yourself and others.

Nearly fifteen years ago, I took Gigi to JH Ranch in the mountains of Northern California. If your kids are still young enough and not out of high school yet, I cannot recommend highly enough the experience that awaits you as a mom or dad when attending a week of camp with your son and/or daughter.[1]

JH Ranch is built on the spiritual foundation of how our relationship with God and our love for Jesus will be tested in life. When those tests come—and they will—we must remain steadfast in our obedience and trust. To underscore this principle in real time, the parent and child engage in a number of physical activities, some of which are very challenging.

Examples are whitewater rafting, huge rope swings over a lake, high tightrope walks, and blindfolded walks in the forest. Then there was the one where we were supposed to jump from one of two high cliffs into a pool of extremely cold, swirling mountain

1 Check out www.jhranch.com.

water. Regarding the latter challenge, I knew that Gigi, being on the autism spectrum, would have a tough time making the jump from even the lower cliff—about twenty-five feet high—because she has significant visual and spatial issues as well as anxiety.

On a hot summer afternoon, we hiked for an hour with a group of about fifty into the woods until we reached the river.

"That's where we're jumping from," said our guide, pointing to a cliff overlooking a pool of water that looked the size of a postage stamp.

Oh, my goodness! I looked toward Gigi. Fear was written all over her face. I tried to hide mine.

We didn't *have* to jump, but that was the whole point of the hike, right?

"Tell you what, Gigi," I said. "I'll go up there and check it out. Does that sound like a good idea to you?"

"A great idea," my daughter agreed.

I followed the first group up the cliff to the higher jump, which was steeper than expected. When I got to the top, I turned around. The water—the landing zone—looked like it was a *long* way down there. Maybe forty feet or about four stories.

I'm not too fond of heights either. But I knew I couldn't let my daughter down—or myself. I watched other girls and their fathers make their way to the cliff's edge. Some hesitated or had to be coaxed to step off, while others grabbed for the gusto and didn't hesitate to launch themselves into the air.

After hitting the water, the typical reaction was this: "It's cold!"

Waiting for my turn was nerve-wracking. Finally, I was close to the head of the line. Just one person in front of me. I looked over the edge and had a bird's eye view of how high we were and how small the cauldron of water looked.

One of the counselors was telling each jumper when it was

time to jump. I decided that when he said it was my turn, I would not hesitate. Otherwise, I would be a goner. I'd never step off.

I jumped into the great unknown but forgot to hold my nose. Big mistake. And the water *was* freezing! But I survived, and my pride was intact.

Gigi saw me jump, of course. She really didn't want to jump, especially from the higher one, so I said, "Let's go together up to the lower jump." This gave her some breathing room.

By now, the number of dads and daughters lining up to jump from either spot was thinning. It was apparent that every adult and teen would make the jump from one of the heights.

"Sure," she said. "Let's do this."

I carefully assisted a very scared but game Gigi up the rocks and out to the edge of a slippery rock at the lower jump. She rocked back and forth with the motion of someone who wanted to jump but couldn't pull the trigger as she looked over the edge, as had all the others before her.

"You can do this. I know you can," I said soothingly. I was encouraging my daughter, knowing that, with her visual and spatial deficits, the jump must have looked like Niagara Falls to her.

This coaxing and encouragement went on for about fifteen minutes as she stepped aside each time someone else wanted to make the plunge. This happened until everyone was at the river's edge, looking up at Gigi and me. She was feeling the pressure to jump, and I'm certain she was weighing what it would be like *not* to jump and having to carefully make her way back down a steep and slippery cliff.

Then a chorus of voices rose in unison from the forest below.

"You got this, Gigi."

"God has you, girl."

"You can do this, Gigi."

Many, many more voices joined in the chorus of encouragement that flowed upward from the river to our ears.

In those forever unforgettable moments, I felt like a choir of angels had surrounded us. *This is what heaven must feel like* . . . nothing but love filled the air. The power of their encouragement from those who, only a few days before, were total strangers must have been overwhelming for Gigi, because she . . . jumped.

Seeing her struggle upon hitting the water, I immediately sailed into the air after her—and landed just a bit to the side of her. After I hit the cold water and rose to the surface, I searched for my daughter. She was struggling, still scared by her surroundings. I immediately came to her side and assisted her to a sandy spot along the river. As we exited the water, I could tell my daughter was proud of her accomplishment. She had done it!

You see, when Gigi jumped, she didn't just jump for herself. She stepped off the ledge and leaped for herself and her family—present and future—and she leaped for all who'd encouraged her that day. She has been even braver since then, even jumping out of an airplane! I realized that day how powerful words can be to encourage others to take a leap of faith and how those words can transcend generations. As Scripture says:

> Death and life are in the power of the tongue,
> and those who love it will eat its fruit.
>
> —Proverbs 18:21 (ESV)

Statistically, if we each change ten people's lives for the better and they each change ten other lives for the better and so on, within a few generations, more than 100,000 people will have a better view of themselves and others.

We can be inspired by the One who set the bar on what real friendship is. When Jesus Christ went to the Cross and died the death we should have experienced, He paid the price for our sins. There's no greater love than that. He died to pay the debt we should have paid and to set our hearts free. No higher bar can be set for pure, selfless love.

God did not distinguish for whom He died. He was ready to give the keys to heaven to those who tortured Him and would ultimately kill Him. "Father, forgive them for they know not what they do" (Luke 23:34, ESV), He said from the Cross.

Surely, there is nothing of the magnitude of wrong committed against the innocent Jesus that we have or will experience that we cannot forgive in others. Consider these verses:

> For Christ also suffered once for our sins, the righteous for the unrighteous, to bring you to God.
>
> —1 PETER 3:18 (NIV)

> In this is love, not that we have loved God, but that he loved us and sent his Son to be the propitiation for our sins. Beloved, if God so loved us, we also ought to love one another.
>
> 1 JOHN 4:10-11 (ESV)

This friendship with Jesus is based on a transformed life, a new life, not the old ways of thinking. What He did on the Cross for each and all of us should always be in our thoughts and drive our actions. When we have that mindset, our lives are marked by profound humility, unsullied purity, and complete devotion to God. It's nothing short of supernatural as now there almost always seems to be time for an act of kindness to extend to someone else. We should show grace to others as He has shown us His grace.

It's like a little ditty I wrote:

> "Grace beyond what we understand,
> For fallen man now holds God's hand."

Never forget that God's purpose is that the glory of His Son be manifested in our mortal flesh, which is why we need to guard our hearts because everything flows from it.

You will know if your life's perspective is changing for the better if other people's needs are becoming more important than your own. You'll know you're on the right track when the worldly things that had a grip on you become less important.

Are you ready to be more than you are today?

The first commandments were written on stone tablets. On the night before Jesus went to the Cross, He gave us a new commandment that should be inscribed on our hearts:

> "A new commandment I give you, that you love one another: just as I have loved you, you are also to love one another. By this all will know that you are My disciples, if you have love for one another."
>
> —JOHN 13:34-35 (ESV)

If He is in you, are you paying attention to what comes out of you? Then consider these ten benefits to the giver of kindness:

1. Kindness makes you happier.
2. Kindness is good for the physical health of your heart.
3. Kindness slows aging.
4. Kindness improves your relationships.
5. Kindness is contagious.

6. Kindness supports your immune system.
7. Kindness releases feel-good hormones.
8. Kindness supports mental health.
9. Kindness eases anxiety.
10. Kindness reduces stress.[1]

"Anyone who withholds kindness from a friend forsakes the fear of the Almighty," says Job 6:14 (NIV). When you extend kindness to others because Jesus loves you, you will likely receive way more than you give. It's the cosmic way of Christianity—and a completely upward spiral.

It's been said that we only live once, but if it's a life well lived, once is enough. That means your life was rich in friendships and kindness as well.

This week, be the best divine version of yourself. Bring that Divinity to a waiting world. Be a friend to someone you know and to someone new.

You won't regret the effort.

1 From the editors at BrightVibes.com.

6

Are You Ready to Become Like a Little Child?

Jesus called a little child to him and put the child among them. Then he said, "I tell you the truth, unless you turn from your sins and become like little children, you will never get into the Kingdom of Heaven. So, anyone who becomes as humble as this little child is the greatest in the Kingdom of Heaven."

—MATTHEW 18:2-4 (NLT)

Here are some questions to consider as we get going.

- **What is childlike behavior?**
- **What is childish behavior?**
- What kind of behavior does the world promote?
- What kind of behavior does Jesus promote?
- **Why does Jesus place such significance on being childlike?**

Oswald Chambers, author of *My Utmost for the Highest*, shared some insights:

> The complete life is the life of the child . . . The child of God is not conscious of the will of God because he is the will of God . . . A child of God never prays to be conscious that God answers prayer, he is so restfully certain that God always answers prayer. . . Whenever Jesus comes, he establishes rest . . .

I don't believe there is a neurotypical adult who isn't enamored with a child's innocence, the focus of this chapter.

I can still remember shopping at a local grocery store many years ago. I was standing in the produce section when I heard a couple of girls giggling a couple of aisles over. The snickering was so infectious that I smiled and was drawn to see where the giggling came from.

I pushed my shopping cart toward the merriment and spotted two girls, probably ten years old, standing in the aisle and laughing hysterically at one another's stories.

What was so funny? I didn't know, and it didn't matter. I realized these two girls were caught up in the moment and didn't care who saw them or what anyone else thought. They were laughing at seemingly nothing because of their vivid imaginations and playful natures.

I wondered when the last time I had been in a playful mood or had a good laugh was. *Too long*, I decided.

Interestingly, Jesus said certain childlike behaviors and attitudes must be carried through adulthood and even up to death.

His teaching runs up against the natural side of life, the part where children can't wait to become "unchildlike." You see it when preschool kids are asked their age. One might hold up three fingers and say, "Three and a half," or another might proudly declare, "I'm almost five."

Each statement is declared with the determination of someone who wants to grow up quickly. We all felt that way as we discovered our surroundings.

That's why I find it interesting that the world has done an incredible job of forcing adulthood on us while promoting childish behavior rather than encouraging us to become adults and carry the positive attributes of childhood.

Why is that?

Because childish behavior is all about the self and satisfying the self. This is not the "childlike" behavior Jesus is referring to.

The *Merriam-Webster Dictionary* defines "childish" as someone marked by immaturity and a lack of poise; someone who avoids responsibility and seeks attention; and someone who isn't afraid to use shame, guilt, fear, or manipulation to get what he or she wants.

Meanwhile, the *Oxford Dictionary* defines "childlike"—for an adult—as having the qualities associated with children, such as trust, innocence, directness, unsophistication, simplicity, and honesty. They act without deception.

So, given the childish nature of many in the world today, as evidenced by the *Merriam-Webster* definition, it would seem the world is doing a pretty darn good job of promoting self-centered, selfish, and "it's all about me" behavior instead of being childlike.

So, just what kind of childish behavior does the world encourage?

American psychologist Abraham Maslow theorized our actions are motivated by a "hierarchy of needs," which are listed here in order of priority:

1. Physiological needs are the biological requirements for human survival, such as food, drink, shelter, clothing, warmth, and sleep.
2. Safety needs are security, predictability, and control in our lives after our physiological needs have been met.
3. Love and belonging needs refer to the human emotional need for personal relationships and connecting with others. This need comes forth after the physiological and safety needs have been met.
4. Self-esteem needs refer to the idea of self-value, accomplishment, and respect for others.
5. Self-actualization needs describe the fulfillment of your full potential as a person.

Regarding the last need, Maslow was a secular humanist who believed that people had an inborn desire to be self-actualized, or, said another way, to be all they can be and find their way through their own efforts. Before that can happen, several basic needs must be met, including food, safety, love, and self-esteem.

Maslow placed self-actualization at the top of his pyramid of the hierarchy of needs for a reason—the idea that realizing one's full potential deserves the supreme position in our lives. The only problem with this approach is that it sets everyone up to be their own little "gods," defining what is right for themselves without regard for a higher moral order.

We all want to be the best we can be, but can't self-actualization be achieved by fulfilling God's purpose for our lives? The answer is yes, it can. Jesus' desire is for everyone to be all they were divinely designed to be and to be one with Him and the Father (John 17:22). Loving God and serving others seems like a great way to go through life instead of the relentless pursuit of self-satisfaction, which is worldly self-actualization and not the divine self-actualization that comes from putting Jesus first and others second.

Theologian Oswald Chambers made this observation:

> Our Lord's teaching is always anti-self-realization. His purpose isn't to develop our personal qualities. It's to make us exactly like him—and his chief characteristic is self-sacrifice.

God spilled the life of His Son so that the world might be saved. Are we ready to spill out our lives for Him?

As a society, the truth must be stated: we've run roughshod over some critical interpersonal dynamics on our way to defining self-actualization so shallowly.

Without a doubt, the introduction of the selfie is one of the great modern gateways to all the dysfunction around us and the dissolution existing between people today. The ability to take photographs of ourselves on our smartphones and post them on social media or share them with others has ushered in an era of constantly turning attention to oneself.

There are plenty of studies these days showing that selfies promote narcissism, create unrealistic physical expectations, and harm one's self-esteem. This tireless focus on self and the pressure to present a perfect image to the world increases anxiety and symptoms of depression, especially if one doesn't receive a certain number of Facebook likes!

This would be an excellent time to be reminded that the Bible has many passages describing what God has to say about our real worth and personal value to Him:

> Then God said, "Let us make human beings in our image, to be like us."
>
> —GENESIS 1:26 (NLT)

That's nothing short of mind-blowing, knowing that we are made in God's very image, the very likeness of God. Since it's true, wouldn't God's Word be worth investigating at a much deeper level?

In Psalms, we're reminded that we are fearfully and wonderfully made and told that all the days of our lives were written in God's book before we were ever born, confirming God's prior knowledge of who we are and that He has a plan for our lives:

> You made all the delicate, inner parts of my body
> and knit me together in my mother's womb.
> Thank you for making me so wonderfully complex!
> Your workmanship is marvelous—how well I know it.
> You watched me as I was being formed in utter seclusion,
> as I was woven together in the dark of the womb.
> You saw me before I was born.
> Every day of my life was recorded in your book.
> Every moment was laid out
> before a single day had passed.
>
> —PSALM 139:13-16 (NLT)

On the other hand, the world continues to propel itself into an ever-deeper hole of **self-redemption and self-reliance**. At the same time, the ties that used to bind us together as individuals and as a homogeneous society are fraying to the point of breaking. That's because we look to ourselves and others for our self-worth—instead of looking to the One who created us for our self-worth. When we keep our focus on Jesus, that's when we begin to realize our full potential.

So, let me pose a question:

Can we continue to anesthetize ourselves with the glorification of self to shield ourselves from the chaos continuously hitting us between the eyes?

I think not. We are train wrecks waiting to happen—if they haven't happened already for many of us.

This overarching confluence of powerful media influences is coming at us from all sides, making it increasingly difficult for human beings to think beyond their self-prescribed versions of what is right and wrong. This is not sustainable.

Let's take a good look around us. Are things working out well in terms of people showing more kindness to one another? Is there a fullness of peace and unity in the land? Given the concentration of wealth in fewer and fewer people, the glorification of self through social media, and the temporal ornaments the world adorns for those who fight the hardest for their piece of the proverbial pie, it's clear that true godly purposes are more distant than ever.

I remember one cover of *Surfing* magazine some time ago when Kelly Slater, probably the greatest surfer of all time, was surrounded by a pack of a hundred extremely high-caliber surfers at the famous Pipeline surf break in Hawaii. A big swell came in, and Kelly was pictured dropping into a wave perfectly poised and positioned among a sea of other surfers. The cover headline read: "Cutting through the clutter."

Slater caught a great wave because he was ready—in the right place at the right time (and it didn't hurt to be Kelly Slater). It takes time and effort to make the right choices and not be sucked into what the world tells you is right and wrong. Each of us must find the right spot and pick our way through the clutter.

Let's return to what Jesus had to say about childlike behavior. In Matthew 19:14 (NLT), when the disciples were pushing the children away from Jesus, Jesus said:

> "Let the children come to me. Don't stop them! For the Kingdom of Heaven belongs to those who are like these children." And he placed his hands on their heads and blessed them before he left.

Wow . . . that sounds super important! And in Mark 10:15 (NLT), Jesus said:

> "I tell you the truth, anyone who doesn't receive the Kingdom of God like a child will never enter it."

Whoa! We *must* pay attention to this directive from the One True Caregiver about childlike behavior so we are ready to meet Him one day.

Our culture and all major religions other than Christianity boil down to this proclamation: *If I do this, then I get that.* Only Christianity—where God reached down to planet Earth to give us His only son, Jesus Christ, who shed His blood and died to pay the price for our sins—says that if we accept with childlike faith what He did for us, then we will enter into His kingdom for eternity.

Remember this key verse:

> But God showed his great love for us by sending Christ
> to die for us while we were still sinners.
>
> —Romans 5:8 (NLT)

The gift of all gifts must be simply received with childlike humility. There's really no other way. Our good works, whatever they may be, are not a scorecard we present to God with the hope that He will give us a passing grade and accept us. Our good works are a *response* to our understanding that He has already given us everything!

One of many encouraging outcomes of having a childlike faith is found in 1 Peter 5:7 (NIV):

> Cast all your anxiety on Him because he cares for you.

Worldly childish behavior can make us fearful of what others may do to us, which could cause us to retreat from doing what we know is right in our daily pursuit to provide for ourselves and those we love and care about.

Hebrews 13:5-6 (NLT) says:

> Don't love money; be satisfied with what you have.
> For God has said,
> "I will never fail you.
> I will never abandon you."
> So we can say with confidence,
> "The Lord is my helper,
> so I will have no fear.
> What can mere people do to me?"

In a similar vein, Proverbs 29:25 says:

> Fearing people is a dangerous trap,
> but trusting the Lord means safety.

As dependent children of the King, we need not fear our social status. We need not fear our bank account balance. We need not fear what others may think of us.

We *do* need to ask ourselves if the Son of God is being allowed full reign within us because everything in the world is clamoring to put the Son of God to death in us. We will have to fight this battle until our last day on earth.

Does Jesus' innocence, purity, and simplicity have time to manifest itself in us? That is the question we must ask ourselves every day.

Jesus Christ lived among regular men and women with all their faults, foibles, and sins. Yet He lived a virtuous, sinless, and simple life with a consistent retreat for prayer time with His Father.

The takeaway: Prayer changes us so we can change things.

It's not hyperbole to say that His life was the most exemplary ever lived. I often wonder what this planet would be like if everyone used Jesus as *the* example to go about their lives.

Driving toward the beach recently, I watched a group of young schoolchildren walking on the sidewalk. They must have been going somewhere because they were gleefully skipping and hopping, wearing their hats to shield themselves from the sun, lovingly cocooned by their teachers in front and back.

Several children looked at the cars and trucks passing by

and laughed as they pumped their arms up and down, hoping to get a honk.

More than a few drivers obliged. As horns honked, their laughter increased, prompting a smile in my heart at witnessing simple, unadulterated pleasure and joy in the moment. Those kids did something innocuous but probably set the tone for the rest of the day—have fun!

So, when was the last time you pumped your arm to a big rig driver to get him to hit his horn?

A long time ago, right?

The next time you pass a truck on the freeway, pump your arm and see what happens. You *both* might have a fun moment when the truck driver blasts his horn.

Which brings me to a final thought: How do you know you're growing in the Lord and becoming more childlike?

Well, you're more accepting of your shortcomings.

You realize you don't need to know it all.

You're not concerned about having advantages over others.

You're less anxious about the future.

You're more concerned about others than yourself.

You're more accepting of others.

This week, regardless of your age, display a childlike joy and faith and prove the world wrong.

7

Are You Ready to Stop Spinning So Many Plates?

work: *to perform or fulfill duties regularly for wages or salary; to perform or carry through a task requiring sustained effort or continued repeated operations; to exert oneself physically or mentally, especially in a sustained effort for a purpose or under compulsion or necessity.*

—*Merriam-Webster Dictionary*

Many years ago, families gathered around their twenty-seven-inch black-and-white television sets to watch a variety show on Sunday nights called *The Ed Sullivan Show*.

As a kid growing up in the Sixties, I loved lying on the floor in front of the living room TV and watching the hour-long program with my family. *The Ed Sullivan Show* featured a variety of acts—singers, music groups, comedians, contortionists, and what have you—that made for must-watch TV, including the Beatles' first nationwide appearance on February 9, 1964. Watching John, Paul, George, and Ringo sing "All My Loving" and

"She Loves You" was tremendously exciting as a ten-year-old.

One of the novelty acts I looked forward to watching was Erich Brenn, otherwise known as the "plate spinner." He'd come on stage and stand next to a table with a stack of dinner plates and a bunch of long poles. He'd set one plate spinning on top of one of the poles, then another, and another, until a dozen plates were spinning at once. From the corner of his eye, he'd spot a plate starting to slow and wobble. Brenn would dash over to the wobbly plate and furiously spin it up to speed again—before making a mad dash to the next plate that was close to running out of rotations. Watching Brenn race around the table was entertaining but also anxiety-provoking as he hustled from one end to the other to keep all the dinner plates spinning in the air.[1]

Plate spinning was a classic vaudeville skill in which plates and bowls were kept spinning, balanced, and rotating on poles without falling. During the 1950s and 1960s, Erich Brenn became famous for his plate-spinning act, which he elevated into high drama and comedy as he frantically dashed from plate to plate, giving them a quick spin and keeping everything going. I loved watching this novelty act.

1 You can watch Erich Brenn spin his plates on *The Ed Sullivan Show* by going to YouTube and using these search words: Erich Brenn Ed Sullivan Show.

The plate spinner reminds me of how our work life can unfold each day. In our never-ending effort to complete more and more items on our To-Do list, it can often feel like we're running from one wobbly spinning plate to another. The feeling of never catching up usually drives us into a deep sense of foreboding regarding whether we will ever accomplish everything we think we should or must. And so goes our daily lives, revolving around our work and how we make a living.

So what is "work"? Many people have offered their definitions. Here are some of my favorites:

> "Work is effort applied towards some end. The most satisfying work involves directing our efforts toward achieving ends that we ourselves endorse as worthy expressions of our talent and character."
>
> —WILLIAM J. BENNETT, former US Secretary of Education and author of *The Book of Virtues*

> "Most people work just hard enough not to get fired and get paid just enough money not to quit."
>
> —comedian GEORGE CARLIN

> "Work is an extension of personality. It is an achievement. It is one of the ways in which a person defines himself, measures his worth, and his humanity."
>
> —PETER F. DRUCKER, author of *Management: Tasks, Responsibilities, Practices*

> "By working faithfully eight hours a day, you may eventually get to be boss and work twelve hours a day."
>
> —poet ROBERT FROST

> "When work is a pleasure, life is a joy. When work is a duty, life is slavery."
>
> —MAXIM GORKY, author of *The Lower Depths*

The Bible teaches that from the very beginning, God created us to work. He said to Adam:

> "Be fruitful and multiply and fill the earth and subdue it, and have dominion over the fish of the sea and over the birds of the heavens and over every living thing that moves on the earth."
>
> —GENESIS 1:28 (ESV)

God also gave Adam a job to do:

> The Lord God took the man and put him in the garden of Eden to work it and keep it.
>
> —GENESIS 2:15 (ESV)

In other words, work began as an excellent thing in the Garden and was part of a significant and perfect communal relationship with God.

Although God ordained work for mankind from the very beginning, the work God ordained then was not like the work of today.

When sin entered the world through the rebellious actions of both Adam and Eve, God evicted the pair from paradise. That's when work became cursed by God since it reflected the stain of sin.

God addressed this in Genesis when He spoke directly to Adam:

> "Because you have listened to the voice of your wife
> and have eaten of the tree
> of which I commanded you,

> 'You shall not eat of it,'
> cursed is the ground because of you;
> in pain you shall eat of it all the days of
> your life;
> thorns and thistles it shall come forth for you;
> and you shall eat the plants of the field.
> By the sweat of your face
> you shall eat bread,
> till you return to the ground,
> for out of it you were taken;
> for you are dust,
> and to dust you shall return."
>
> —GENESIS 3:17-19 (ESV)

And for good measure, He also said this:

> "When you work the ground, it shall no longer yield to you its strength."
>
> —GENESIS 4:12A (ESV)

So, since the great "falling apart," work has been a paradox. Labor, which God originally ordained as good, can still be that way if undertaken with the right approach. However, work incorporates the curse, as evidenced by the myriad situations in which people suffer because of how they approach work.

When work is not approached as God intended it from the beginning, toiling for our daily bread can negatively affect marriages, family members, and other relationships. A very high percentage of divorce, substance abuse, crime, depression, and suicide result from work-related issues.

It's time to take a fresh look at how work can overtake our lives. We must find a balance between God-given ambition and God-ordained contentment.

Today, people work an average of eight to twelve hours a day. Nearly two-thirds of Americans aged sixteen or older work.

Almost everyone has to work to support themselves and their dependents, at least until retirement age. But even then, tons of people work in their late sixties and seventies, either by choice or because they must make money to survive.

According to the Bible, God rested after six days of work. Today, most people cannot find the time or afford to rest for a couple of hours a week, let alone an entire day. On top of that, most people dislike their jobs and barely get through an eight-hour shift. That's too bad because work should be incredibly meaningful for them and those around them.

The Sabbath is in the Bible for a reason: if God Himself rested on the last day of creation, then He was sending a strong

What happened to Sunday walks and stopping to enjoy a picturesque view from a wooden bench? It's a shame that the traditional Sabbath—a day dedicated to rest, reflection, and restoration—has faded for too many folks.

message that we need to do the same for our refreshment and restoration. That's why I'm pleased when I hear stories—which are growing more numerous by the day—of those putting their phones down, turning off their computers for a full twenty-four hours, and rediscovering parts of themselves, their families, and their friends for at least one day a week.

Oswald Chambers summed it up well in *My Utmost for His Highest*:

> Self-realization leads to the enthronement of work, whereas the believer enthrones Jesus in his work.

Thankfully, God already had a plan for reconstruction and restoration through a relationship with Jesus Christ. When we commit our hearts to Jesus, we receive a new playbook for all aspects of life—including work:

> Whatever you do, work heartily, as for the Lord and not for men, knowing that from the Lord you will receive the inheritance as your reward. You are serving the Lord Jesus Christ.
>
> —Colossians 3:23-24 (NIV)

The Bible also reminds us that our work can have a meaningful temporal value and can also be of eternal value and glorifying to God:

> Commit your works to the Lord,
> and your plans will be established.
>
> —Proverbs 16:3 (ESV)

God took man and put him in the Garden of Eden to work and take care of it. It's a pity that Adam, who took a bite of the forbidden fruit when offered by his helpmate Eve, blew up that good deal.

The bottom line is work is blessed, but as I've already noted, work is also cursed. That's how things will be until we are set free permanently from the corruption that entered all of us after Adam and Eve sinned.

Until that happens, we need not burn ourselves out to the uttermost ends of physical exhaustion. Instead, we can play a meaningful part in the great restoration that is coming through our renewed approach to work. Let this Scripture sustain you:

> Cast your cares on the Lord,
> and he will sustain you;
> He will never permit
> the righteous to be moved.
>
> —Psalm 55:22 (ESV)

So, you must ask yourself: Are you ready to approach work differently as the present quickly becomes the past?

The problem with work is that it's seen as a means to an end when it could be a fulfilling way to live.

For most, work is a means to an elusive end, which is understandable because of the financial pressures on families and individuals, no matter who's in power in Washington. Seventy-eight percent of people in America today live paycheck to paycheck, meaning nearly four-fifths of households are a one-car breakdown from absolute financial straits, according to a Payroll.org survey taken in 2023. When you're living paycheck to paycheck, it's nearly impossible to save any money, let alone invest for the future. You're even more vulnerable in times of emergency.

It's hard to have any sort of work-life balance when there's often more month than money. I remember the first time I experienced a healthy work-life balance—defined as maintaining a harmonious relationship between work and personal life—during a surfing trip to Australia many years ago.

Whenever I walked into a pub with my new mates, I noticed that local TV news programs showed five or ten minutes of news, then spent the rest of the hour showing highlights of rugby, cricket, soccer, tennis, and Australian Rules Football. Now, that's what I call a great work-life balance!

After traveling for a month Down Under, I was convinced that every Australian male was born with a fishing pole in one hand and a surfboard in the other. Australians take their time off and outdoor time seriously, as reflected in their paid vacation policies. Most Australian employees *start* with four weeks of paid vacation each year and have generous sick, maternity, paternity, bereavement, and even voting leave. There are seven legal national holidays observed in each state. That sounds like a better balance between work and rest than what is happening in America.

Think of how much better off we'd be with a better work-life balance, but we Americans tend to be fearful of the repercussions of taking our foot off the work accelerator. We fear what will happen if we stop working so hard. The net result is we're unable to enjoy the vacation and weekend days given to us. Fear and anxiety live in the past and the future. That is definitely not where we want to live.

The world wants work to be a primary idol—a "little g" god that acts as a conduit to all the worldly adornments constantly flashing in front of our eyes. Never mind the harsh reality that most of those "wants" will most likely never be in our possession. Nonetheless, precious time is lost in the pursuit.

We are a nation of shopaholics and continuous consumption. Over-shopping only fuels the meaningless fire of self-fulfillment.

It doesn't help matters when we're inundated by endless social media posts from "influencers" projecting what we need to be happy—new outfits, new shoes, new friends, new restaurants, new cars, and new places to travel to. When we buy into this lie, we open ourselves to disappointments about how we look, what we wear, where we live, and where we travel. The world does not preach contentment and graciousness—and never has.

The focus on self-fulfillment and self-aggrandizement—defined as drawing attention to your own importance—leads to purchasing things we don't need with money we don't have to impress people we don't know. We're conditioned to buy the latest and greatest smartphone, gizmo, hot clothing brand, or expensive handbag because . . . everyone else is.

This quest for consumerism plays right into Satan's hands. He wants us to be distracted, deluded, and in debt from pursuing the latest shiny bauble. While there's nothing inherently wrong with most of the shiny objects of the world, most people are looking in the wrong place for the happiness they seek.

The problem with the world's idols is that they will always let us down. The depth of the hurt we will experience from the fall of those disappointments will be directly related to the height of the pedestal where we placed that false god.

Remember this admonition from the apostle John:

> Little children, keep yourself from idols.
>
> —1 John 5:21 (ESV)

What's interesting about this short sentence is that it's the final verse from John's first letter. He's not literally talking to "little children" but refers to adults like you and me with an admonishment to stop chasing false gods. John must have felt strongly about teaching this since he saved this rebuke until the very end of his epistle.

When I started the real estate development portion of my career nearly thirty years ago, I was working in Montana. We had made many trips there over the years and discovered that we loved exploring Big Sky Country.

One time, my wife, Catherine, and I took our youngest daughter, Gigi, to Whitefish, a lovely resort town twenty-five miles from the entrance to Glacier National Park.

While we were walking through the picturesque village and peeking into various local stores, which we always love to do, Catherine found a wooden sign—four feet wide and about eight inches tall—that she liked, saying it would be perfect for our home. In a few words, this touristy sign spoke volumes about the way my wife felt about my work life at the time:

Enjoy this moment . . .
This moment is your life

That sign has hung over various doors in our home for years and never failed to do two things:

1. Remind me to appreciate how wise my wife is.
2. Never forget how truthful and impactful those words were to me.

Decades later, as I look back on a career that took me far from those Glacier Park trails, the words still hang above a doorway in our home—and in my heart. They continue to pull me back to what matters most: Enjoy this moment . . . this moment is your life.

Because, in the end, those accumulated moments are part of the foundation Catherine and I built, resting on the true cornerstone: Jesus Christ.

Working can also create problems with comparison. The world is full of people overloaded with stuff who think they should accumulate even more goods. That's a shame because they're transacting in the world's economy, not God's. These words from Jesus should be our guiding light:

> "Take care, and be on your guard against all covetousness, for one's life does not consist in the abundance of his possessions."
>
> —Luke 12:15 (ESV)

In the book of John, Jesus discusses with Peter—after the Resurrection—what He wants Peter to do. After saying, "Feed my sheep," Jesus added this to Peter:

> "Truly, truly, I say to you, when you were young, you used to dress yourself and walk wherever you wanted, but when you are old, you will stretch out your hands, and another will dress you and carry you where you do not want to go." (This he said to show by what kind of death he was to glorify God.)
>
> —JOHN 21:18-19 (ESV)

Peter then turned toward the apostle John and said to Jesus:

> "Lord, what about this man?" Jesus said to him, "If it is my will that he remain until I come, what is that to you? You follow me!"
>
> —JOHN 21:21-22 (ESV)

Besides intimating to Peter that he would die for Him someday, Jesus also demonstrated that God uniquely designed us with a special plan for our lives. Comparison with others is a futile and counterproductive behavior.

We cannot live the abundant life Jesus promised us if we crowd Him out with stuff.

I believe anxiety is the soundtrack playing in the background of modern work life.

Persistent worry and fear often lead to a fast heart rate, rapid breathing, sweating, and feeling more tired than we should, which could mean serious health issues. Feeling anxious can prompt us to take shortcuts, jeopardizing the outcomes we want.

There is an old saying, "Nothing good comes from rushing." I found that adage to be personally applicable years ago.

One of our company's first contracts in Montana was to rehabilitate a thirty-four-unit senior complex in the little town of Libby, population 2,775. Our available construction funds did not cover as many items on a punch list as we would have liked, but we accepted the terms anyway. Of particular importance were the building's fire suppression system and a fire notification system directly connected to the Libby Fire Department.

We were not required by law to upgrade the fire suppression system or the connectivity to the Libby Fire Department, but our team chose to do the upgrades anyway and eat the costs.

About a year later, one of the elderly tenants left something burning on the stove in his apartment. This was not an uncommon occurrence in a senior building. His unit caught on fire, triggering the fire suppression system. He also notified the fire department of the fire. Unfortunately, the elderly tenant perished before firefighters could save him.

The silver lining was that, because we had upgraded the fire suppression and notification systems, the fire was quickly contained before any other lives were lost. While certain situations may lend themselves to a shortcut, it's best not to compromise when the safety and health of others are at stake.

So, I have a question for you: Does anything you do each day at work impact the safety or health of others? Even if it does not, you're in a unique position every day. You can positively influence others and potentially impact them for Christ.

Our company was hailed as heroes by those who knew what we did—doing the extra work when it wasn't in the contract. Word got around. For our company, this verse says it all:

> A good name is to be chosen rather than great riches,
> and favor is better than silver and gold.
>
> —Proverbs, 22:1 (ESV)

I shudder to think what would have happened had our company not upgraded Libby's fire suppression system. We need to always thank the Lord for giving us the wisdom to do the right thing, even when it cuts into the bottom line.

Perhaps you're reading this book before your workday begins. Maybe you're winding down before going to bed. There's a good chance that no matter what time of day you're thumbing through *Are You Ready?*, your head is spinning at a hundred miles per hour, thinking about what you need to do next.

Maybe you're ready for a different approach to your work week. I know I had to soul-search over the years about what I valued most or *should* value. My conclusion is that trying to become rich is a futile exercise:

> In the blink of an eye wealth disappears,
> for it will sprout wings
> and fly away like an eagle.
>
> —Proverbs 23:5 (NLT)

Actor and comedian Jim Carrey said this one time: "I think everyone should get rich and famous and do everything they ever dreamed of so they can see that it's not the answer." Sounds like some inner reflection work was done by Mr. Carrey with these well-said words to consider.

Let us not hold too tightly to the things of this world but

extend our hands out, with palms up, and be grateful for everything we have, even if some of what we have is difficult to deal with. Remember this advice from the apostle Paul:

> Rejoice always, pray without ceasing, give thanks in all circumstances; for this is the will of God in Christ Jesus for you.
>
> —1 Thessalonians: 5:16-18 (ESV)

We enter a new plateau of transformational hope when we own this verse—and not just recite it.

We are consistently and not always obviously being watched by others whenever we do business or are in the marketplace. I was reminded of this when we put the Lafayette Hotel in San Diego on the market one time. Several buyers were courting us, including a burly billionaire from the Midwest.

I sat across from him in a small conference room and started with small talk. He told me that he noticed at the bottom of my emails to him that I always included the salutation, "Lead with love; it's universally understood."

The businessman looked at me and chuckled. "I like to lead with a strong left cross," he stated.

I laughed politely at the time—I was trying to close the deal, after all—but afterward, I thought about how many business folks want to deliver a knockout punch in business because it's all about them and not about fairness or leaving anything on the table.

In business, at home, on the basketball court, or wherever healthy competition is, love must be behind all of our motivations so we may please Jesus in all we think, do, and say:

> "In the same way, let your light shine before others, so that they may see your good deeds and glorify your Father in heaven."
>
> —JESUS' WORDS IN MATTHEW 5:16 (NIV)

When we are with Christ, we have the applause of God and give greater focus to others. We develop a new creed that guides our operations. Work is more than making a point, winning the contract, or getting the deal done—it's also about our impact on others in how we treat them.

We want to show others that we're willing to work hard while keeping in mind that our end-of-life bookend—where our legacy lives—should include many people we have worked with and who will miss us for our love, kindness, and generosity in the name of Jesus.

Our impact goes beyond the eight, ten, or twelve hours a day we work, and it's because of the people we affect. When we begin a transformation that makes us "zealous for good works" (Titus 2:14), we become a vessel for honorable use, set apart as holy and valuable to the master of the house, ready for every good work (2 Timothy 2:21). We are always representing our Lord because our ultimate purpose is to manifest Jesus in us.

I wrote this ditty a while back:

> Life is short,
> Gone in a flash.
> Has it just been about the cold hard cash?
> Maybe it's time to drill down inside
> and find a better way to enjoy the ride.

Take some time this week to be still. Ask yourself: Has work ever disappointed you?

If so, how did you respond?

Did you shake your fist at God? Blame others for what happened? Did you self-medicate with drugs or alcohol?

If so, discuss the events with a close friend or a trusted pastor. It's okay to do this. It's okay to learn from one of your wingmen or wingwomen.

Remember, Jesus has this.

Sometimes, it's hard but very important to remember that we work not from the starting line but from the finish line, being victorious in what He has already done.

Let me illustrate this by sharing one of my favorite blocks of Scripture, which comes from the Sermon on the Mount when Jesus said:

> "Don't store up treasures here on earth, where moths eat them and rust destroys them, and where thieves break in and steal. Store your treasures in heaven, where moths and rust cannot destroy, and thieves do not break in and steal. Wherever your treasure is, there the desires of your heart will also be . . .
>
> "That is why I tell you not to worry about everyday life—whether you have enough food and drink, or enough clothes to wear. Isn't life more than food, and your body more than clothing? Look at the birds. They don't plant or harvest or store food in barns, for your heavenly Father feeds them. And aren't you far more valuable to him than they are? Can all your worries add a single moment to your life?
>
> "And why worry about your clothing? Look at the lilies of the field and how they grow. They don't work or make their clothing, yet Solomon in all his glory was not dressed as beautifully as they are. And if God cares so wonderfully for wildflowers that are here today and thrown into the fire tomorrow,

> he will certainly care for you. Why do you have so little faith?
>
> "So don't worry about these things, saying, 'What will we eat? What will we drink? What will we wear?' These things dominate the thoughts of unbelievers, but your heavenly Father already knows all your needs. Seek the Kingdom of God above all else, and live righteously, and he will give you everything you need.
>
> "So don't worry about tomorrow, for tomorrow will bring its own worries. Today's trouble is enough for today."
>
> —Matthew 6:19-21, 25-34 (NLT)

Someone once said, "It's not the number of days of our life, but the life in the number of our days." So be encouraged this week at work!

8

Are You Ready for Adversity?

"Adversity is the first path to truth."

—Lord Byron, an English poet in the early 19th century

Work was not the only thing that was turned upside down in the Garden when mankind rebelled against the Creator, and the perfect union between God and all humanity was broken.

So were our relationships with others and with ourselves.

With the world's brokenness come trials and tragedies ranging from minor inconveniences to significant hardships. We have a name for these times: *adversity*. This word speaks to feeling overwhelmed by the sheer volume and intensity of challenges we face daily.

Adversity has been an intrinsic part of the human experience since Eve took a bite of the forbidden fruit and handed it to Adam. Throughout our lives, we face personal difficulties that test our limits: job loss, unexpected bills, financial hits, family drama, unanticipated accidents, painful injuries, and losing a loved one.

I don't think I would have wanted to be around when the Black Plague devastated medieval Europe from 1347 to 1352, killing 25 million people and between 30 percent and 50 percent of the population. During the 20th century, two major wars—World War I and World War II—were sandwiched around the Great Depression in this country. Talk about major adversity that our great-grandparents and grandparents faced.

Closer to our time, the Covid-19 pandemic of 2020 was no day at the beach. Lockdowns. Businesses closing. Unemployment. Social distancing and masks. Perhaps you lost a family member you couldn't visit in the hospital, or maybe you had to deal with this horrible sickness yourself.

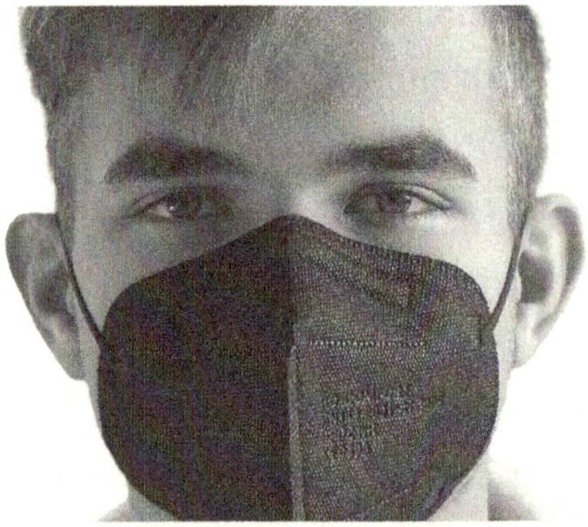

During the height of the Covid-19 lockdowns in the spring of 2020, I—along with everyone else in San Diego—was banned from going to the beach or even going in the water to get a surf session in! Across the country, people couldn't go to neighborhood parks, restaurants, and many other businesses. Scholastic and mental health suffered as well. So unfortunate.

Today, our political climate is marked by significant division and polarization. It's not a stretch to say that we're living in adverse times.

Which leads me to three critical questions we must all ask ourselves:

1. What is adversity?
2. What is the world's approach to adversity?
3. What is Jesus's approach to adversity?

The *Merriam-Webster* dictionary defines adversity as "a state or instance of serious or continued difficulty or misfortune." Adversity can be a conflict within us or a conflict with others.

Professional athletes talk all the time about overcoming adversity. Before a big game or title match, athletes understand that they can control only what they can control—their attitude, emotions, effort, fitness, and preparation. Athletes are coached to not waste time and energy on things they have no control over—weather, field conditions, crowd noise, and refereeing. It's all part of overcoming "adversity" on the field of play or the court.

There is a path to dealing with life's inevitable ups and downs. Similar to the approach I took in the previous chapter regarding the curse of work, I want to present ways we can relate to others and ourselves in a manner that brings us peace in times of trouble.

While significant, life-altering adversity might not strike every day, it's fair to say we encounter smaller forms of adversity or challenges daily.

If you think about it, we experience:

- minor inconveniences like a traffic jam, a spilled cup of coffee, or a frustrating technical glitch.
- personal struggles, such as feeling tired or unmotivated or facing a difficult decision.
- unexpected changes, like a sudden change in plans, an unexpected car repair bill, or a health issue that cropped up. The way we perceive and respond to these daily challenges shapes our resilience and how to handle larger adversities when they arise, which leads me to share these quotes about adversity:

> "Look at a man in the midst of doubt and danger, and you will learn in his hour of adversity what he really is. It is then that the true utterances are wrung from the recesses of his being. The mask is torn off, and reality remains."
>
> —LUCRETIUS, a Roman philosopher, one hundred years before the birth of Christ

> "By trying, we can easily learn to endure adversity . . . another man's, I mean.
>
> —MARK TWAIN, a celebrated American writer from the late 19th century

> "Adversity weakens the weak and strengthens the strong."
>
> —ANONYMOUS

> "To overcome difficulties is to experience the full delight of existence."
>
> —ARTHUR SCHOPENHAUER, German philosopher from the early 19th century

I witnessed how a motorcycle rider overcame difficulties to the full delight of his existence during a drive from Santa Barbara to our San Diego home after Christmas break one year.

We were traveling south in the fast lane of the 405 at about 80 miles per hour on a crowded Sunday afternoon through West LA. To my right, in the next lane over, I saw a Harley-Davidson motorcycle coming up and passing me. Riding the bike was a big burly dude wearing a black leather jacket. His long hair flapped in the breeze, gold chains anchored his neck, and his massive arms gripped the high handlebars with authority. After passing me, the distinctive Hells Angels red lettering on the back of the jacket indicated this man was all business.

In front of the biker was a station wagon with a Christmas tree tied to the roof. Since it was a few days after Christmas, the tree was likely on its way to a recycling center. I noticed the vehicle was probably ten car lengths ahead of the biker—a normal distance. But at 80 miles per hour, that span got covered in a couple of seconds.

Suddenly and without warning, the Christmas tree came loose and flew off the back of the station wagon, landing perpendicular across the biker's lane. I eased off the gas immediately to see if the biker would speed up and get in front of me, but he never deviated to the left or right as he came up on the tree in the middle of the lane. Instead of running over the tree, he popped a wheelie and let the back wheel run right through the Christmas tree, splintering branches and sending pine needles everywhere. Then he coolly laid down the front fork and continued speeding along the freeway as if nothing out of the ordinary had happened.

We see nature overcome adversity in its own way too. That was a lesson I learned while on a springtime surfing trip on the Central Coast of California with a dear friend who was an agricultural science major at UC Davis. During the drive home many years ago, I remember driving past a vineyard with many acres of vines yet to produce.

As someone who knows little about farming, the soil looked bone-dry and wasn't suitable for growing grapes. To my surprise, Larry explained that such conditions can be ideal for growing because the vine has to dig deep to find the nutrients and water it needs, often producing grapes that make delicious wine—all from having endured the ordeal of growth.

In our culture, we tend to avoid adversity at all costs or do what we can to make it go away, run from it, or deal with it on our own strength, as in "muscling through" a problem. In other words, since adversity is not part of any plan, it's best to ignore or avoid it. But nothing could be further from the truth. There is much to absorb, learn, and grow from to build a personal faith.

Going through any crisis helps us decide what is essential, what is worth fighting over, what is worth letting go of, and what is ultimately important. Our eyes must remain fixed on the prize of finishing this race called life with honor and a legacy of meaning.

Are you ready to stop feeling crushed under the weight of what lies ahead?

It's human nature to cope because we hope that a solution to our problems is just around the corner. Optimism is always better than pessimism, and hope is a persistent inner feeling that good can prevail.

So, are you ready for the fight of your life and prepared for the inevitable trials that lie ahead—and to see them through the eyes of our Creator?

The fact is, we have become masters of working against our own better nature and duking it out with our better angels. We have bought into the lie that we can be our own God and determine what is best for ourselves in adversarial situations.

And we face a lot of them because the world seems very long on resentment and very short on grace these days. It appears that the *modus operandi* for many people is to:

1. Divide and polarize.
2. Spread misinformation and distrust.
3. Diminish personal responsibility.
4. Encourage apathy and selfishness.
5. Attack the family structure.
6. Distract and desensitize.
7. Undermine spirituality and morality.

The bottom line is that adversity is part of the curse . . . for now. You can run from adversity, but it will always find you. You can make believe adversity isn't there, but it is. You can dress up adversity and call it something else, but it is what it is.

Jesus, on the other hand, experienced firsthand immense adversity, including betrayal, abandonment, and crucifixion. He knows what adversity is all about and told us that trials are a regular part of life for believers:

> "In the world you will have tribulation. But take heart; I have overcome the world."
>
> —JOHN 16:33B (ESV)

His Word says that trials, tribulations, and adversity can be expected until we draw our final breath:

> For we do not wrestle against flesh and blood, but against the rulers, against the authorities, against the cosmic powers over this present darkness, against the spiritual forces of evil in the heavenly places. Therefore take up the whole armor of God, that you may be able to withstand in the evil day and having done all, to stand firm.
>
> —EPHESIANS 6:12-13 (ESV)

Trials can be both episodic and chronic. Acceptance of both is a big key to navigating, as long as our attitudes allow us to seek peace in Him. Despite the certainty of hardship, Jesus offers a source of peace during troubles in the first half of John 16:33 (ESV):

> "I have said these things to you, that in me you may have peace."

To reach a new plateau where we can actually be grateful (which is not the same as being happy) for the inevitable trials in our lives, let me share this awesome verse of Scripture:

> . . . looking to Jesus, the founder and perfecter of our faith, who for the joy [that would be you and me] that was set before Him, endured the cross, despising the shame, and is seated at the right hand of the throne of God.
>
> —HEBREWS 12:2 (ESV)

This Scripture is a reminder that a deep-down acknowledgement of the suffering Jesus, who has proven Himself to be with us in our trials, gives us transformational hope for the future.

On another aspect of adversity, we can all see that the world keeps on creating adverse times by fighting . . . but fighting for what? The apostle James addressed this topic by writing this:

> What causes quarrels and what causes fights among you? Is it not this, that your passions are at war within you? You desire and do not have, so you murder. You covet and cannot obtain, so you fight and quarrel. You do not have, because you do not ask. You ask and do not receive, because you ask wrongly, to spend it on your passions.
>
> You adulterous people! Do you not know that friendship with the world is enmity with God? Therefore whoever wishes to be a friend of the world makes himself an enemy of God. Or do you suppose it is to no purpose that the Scripture says, "He yearns jealously over the spirit that he has made to dwell in us"? But he gives more grace. Therefore it says, "God opposes the proud but gives grace to the humble."
>
> Submit yourselves therefore to God. Resist the devil, and he will flee from you. Draw near to God, and he will draw near to you. Cleanse your hands, you sinners, and purify your hearts, you double-minded. Be wretched and mourn and weep. Let your laughter be turned to mourning and your joy to gloom. Humble yourselves before the Lord, and he will exalt you.
>
> —James 4:1-9 (ESV)

In the times we live, we are encroached upon daily by a sea of "me monsters." I'm talking about the monster where the eye is a capital "I" and the pressure to conform, compare, and trump others is relentless and furious . . . and fueled by endless social media portals.

What happened to the He and the We?

When we turn from the Me to the He and the We, an unfolding triggers an incredible ability to resolve conflicts within ourselves and with others.

Christianity is rooted in grace, mercy, humility, servanthood, and equality—qualities that promote unity and healing, not division and decay.

The world won't tell us this, but we are at our best when we are in complete agreement with God:

> We have peace with God through our Lord Jesus Christ.
>
> —Romans 5:1b (ESV)

We are so used to getting hammered by the world, but every trial presents the opportunity to cave or cleave.

I have some dear friends, Andy and Laurie, who experienced tragedy when their daughter Hattie passed away in their arms at ten months of age. Rather than run from God, they ran *to* God and found strength and comfort in Him, even though they didn't understand why such a tragic event happened. They formed a nonprofit in their daughter's honor, Hattie's House, that provides complimentary temporary housing in apartments to families and friends of patients seeking medical care in San Diego and at Sutter Medical Center in Sacramento.[1]

When trials come—and Scripture promises they'll happen—we can either turn to God or away from Him, but He never turns His back on us.

Without a test, there's no testimony.

Without a mess, there's no message.

Untested faith is faith that can't be trusted. True faith only becomes deeply personal through trials and conflict.

More than a hundred years ago, Scottish evangelist Oswald Chambers said, "Faith is unutterable trust in God, trust which never dreams that He will not stand by us."

We were created for interdependence with God. Sin leaves us independent from God.

Trials provide opportunities to become dependent on God again and set us on a path toward eternal interdependence with our Creator.

This idea became more real to me one afternoon when I got into my truck for my drive home. Before I turned on the ignition, I spotted a grasshopper resting comfortably on the windshield. I didn't want to harm the little guy and was sure the grasshopper would fly off the windshield as soon as the vehicle started moving.

The grasshopper was still there, however, when I pulled out of my parking place and left the office lot. It was still there as I drove through surface streets, but I noticed something:

1 To learn more about Hattie's House and this worthwhile ministry, please visit hattieshouse.org.

the grasshopper spread its legs and dug in firmly to hold its position on my windshield. The grasshopper even stayed there as I turned onto a freeway entrance ramp and revved up the truck to 75 mph.

Once I got off the freeway and stopped at a stop sign, the grasshopper decided his joyride was over. I'll say this for the insect: he sure was trusting.

With complete trust in God, we can see past any problems and stay assured that God loves us and cares for us continually. He reminds us of this quality about Him from His Word many times, including these verses:

> If God is for us, who can be against us?
>
> —Romans 8:31b (ESV)

> Do not be overcome by evil, but overcome evil with good.
>
> —Romans 12:21 (ESV)

> Many are the sorrows of the wicked,
> But steadfast love surrounds the one who trusts in the Lord.
>
> —Psalm 32:10 (ESV)

> "So also you have sorrow now, but I will see you again, and your hearts will rejoice, and no one will take your joy from you."
>
> —Jesus' words in John 16:22 (ESV)

Oswald Chambers said, "The saint never knows the joy of the Lord in spite of tribulation, but because of it." The bedrock of our Christian faith is the unmerited and fathomless marvel of the love of God exhibited on the cross of Calvary that we can never deserve.

This is a powerful truth. It's our response to adversity that truly shapes our journey. I've long believed that the bar of adversity set by Jesus in His agony is one we must look to and cling to in times of adversity. Even though we all know adversity too well, tough times don't have to derail us.

Think of adversity as a river encountering rocks on its path. The stones create turbulence, but the river doesn't necessarily stop flowing; it finds a way around, over, or even carves a new path.

During times of adversity, our response requires us to be brutally honest with ourselves. We can and should approach the Lord and seek Him out in prayer, saying: *You have promised to get me through . . . help me leave behind what is not of You.*

These days, being honest with oneself seems to be in short supply, as chasing false idols and making exaggerated representations of ourselves to impress others is of paramount importance.

What is on the other side of you? What do people really see, feel, and hear from you?

When you place yourself in that position, you might discover that many of your "approaches" do not promote the best you have to offer yourself, others, and the world. This is the time to step up and ask yourself about where you find yourself in life. Here's some encouragement to do that:

> For I, the Lord your God,
>   hold your right hand;
> It is I who say to you, "Fear not,
>   I am the one who helps you."
>
> —Isaiah 41:13 (ESV)

Similarly, when you face challenges, you have the capacity to adapt, learn, and grow because you are complete in Jesus Christ. You lack nothing. You lose all reasons for trying to hang the world's ornaments of meaning on the branches of your life. You are finally free to be all you were created to be.

The "peace that passes all understanding" from Philippians 4:7 isn't a simple absence of conflict or a feeling easily explained. Instead, a profound sense of calm and security transcends our logical reasoning and emotional responses to challenging adversities. It's a peace rooted in a deep trust and connection with the Lord.

The peace that passes all understanding doesn't magically remove the adversity, but it transforms our inner landscape, equipping us with the emotional, mental, and spiritual resources needed to navigate and ultimately overcome the challenges we face. It's a peace that guards our hearts and minds, allowing us to respond to hardship with strength, clarity, and unwavering hope.

That's how you stand strong in the face of adversity!

9

Are You Ready for Real Humility and Holiness?

"The purpose of all virtue is to lead us to union with God."

—St. John of the Cross, a Spanish mystic who lived from 1542 to 1591

Let me start with a trio of questions:

- What is real humility?
- What is holiness?
- Can you have one without the other?

In today's world, there's a tidal wave of "me, myself and I" stuff going on . . . let's call it the MMI syndrome.

I'm not quite sure when this "look at me" attitude started to snowball, as big egos have been around since humans first walked the planet. I will note, though, that there's been an acceleration of self-focus, self-aggrandizement, and plain old selfishness in recent years, fueled by smartphone photos going straight to people's reels on Instagram, Facebook, TikTok, and X.

These days, people love taking selfies for a mix of psychological, social, and technological reasons. A selfie says, *This is me right now—look where I am and what I'm doing*. Receiving "likes" and comments gives people a sense of validation and boosts their self-esteem and confidence.[2]

I have nothing against taking selfies; I've taken a few of myself over the years. Holding your iPhone at arm's length and snapping a photo of yourself doesn't automatically mean you're vain or self-absorbed. It's nice to capture memories, share moments with loved ones, or have fun creating a memorable shot. However, if one takes selfies mainly to seek admiration or likes on social media, it might come across as self-centered, which clashes with the idea of humility.

Humility is often an overlooked trait, especially in today's culture that prioritizes self-promotion and personal branding. While confidence and ambition are valuable, they can sometimes overshadow a humble attitude, which is quieter and less flashy. In short, humility is a powerful trait to have and doesn't get the attention it deserves—nor the credit it merits for keeping our feet on the ground and our heads out of the clouds.

When *Forbes* magazine published an article not too long ago on the Top 10 characteristics of highly admired people, humility was ranked No. 1. What a nice thing to see. I thought the following paragraphs in the *Forbes* story wonderfully distilled the importance of humility:

---

2 Taking selfies can go too far. Hundreds of people have died in selfie-related accidents—on cliffs, near waterfalls, on train tracks, on rooftops, and even with wild animals. In India, a thirty-eight-year-old man jumped into a lion enclosure to take a selfie with a lion named Dungapur. The lion didn't care that the visitor was angling for an Instagram post. The wild animal attacked the man, dragged him across the enclosure, and mauled him within minutes. The man died at the scene.

> Humility is understood as the ability to accept and love ourselves the way we are, without pretensions. Without hiding the flaws, neither the blessings. With a full understanding of our own strengths and weaknesses. Humility, as is often thought, is not about a low view of one's importance or poor living standards. Humility is about self-awareness and self-management.
>
> Humble people are incredibly attractive. They are empowered and alluring because they have managed to love themselves, and self-confidence is powerful. They are charming because they do not look over anybody's shoulder. Not even when they are greater than everybody else. They are engaging because they do not pretend they are perfect. They accept their limitations and focus on self-improvement.

I would have thought that the rise of selfishness and the divisive political landscape over the last decade had caused humility to fall far below No. 1 in most people's minds. But that didn't happen. I do think, however, that today's pressure-cooker existence, the ever-increasing cost of living, and the striving and competition for meaning in one's life have distracted us. We've collectively taken our eye off the ball, and it shows up in our look-at-me culture, not from what we intuitively know is pleasing, but as **a significant deviation that has sacrificed the good in most of us for what could be the best in all of us.**

What's it going to take to claw our way back to real humility and a more straightforward approach to living? I'll share a few ideas in this chapter that may help guide the way.

Merriam-Webster defines humility as "freedom from pride or arrogance: the quality or state of being humble." Synonyms include meekness, modesty, and down-to-earthiness.

I contend that humility is a foundational element for true holiness. Humility opens the heart to God's grace, which is essential for holiness, a word that's generally defined as the state of being morally and spiritually pure, set apart, or dedicated to God for a higher purpose.

It seems clear that humility is a very positive trait, while holiness is almost otherworldly and ethereal. The question I have is this: **Can people still be holy today? Can holiness become a part of our personal world?**

The answers are yes and yes. In the Bible, holiness isn't just about being morally perfect. It means *being set apart for God*. The Old Testament shows God as holy, as Someone utterly unique, pure, and set apart. He calls His people to "be holy, for I am holy" (1 Peter 1:16). In the New Testament, true holiness does not come from human effort but through Christ making us holy by saving faith, then calling us to live out that holiness daily by growing ever closer to God in love, integrity, and obedience.

Major Ian W. Thomas, British evangelist and founder of Torchbearers Bible schools, shared this insight from his devotional, *The Indwelling Life of Christ*:

> The Christian life is nothing less than the life which Jesus lived . . . now lived by Him in you . . . profoundly simple and simply profound . . . His indwelling is indispensable so that He might accomplish His purposes through us.

Taken as a whole, holiness means being set apart for God and living in a way that reflects purity, reverence, love, and obedience to His divine will. Holiness involves moral integrity, compassion, and a heart aligned with God's purposes. Holiness isn't just about avoiding sin. It's also being transformed and living in a way that reflects God's character.

Many pastors have said that our walk on planet Earth is not about our comfort but about our character, that life is not about our happiness but about our holiness. Those are true and inspirational words to think about.

So, what is the world's view of humility and holiness?

Humility is valued around the globe, but its understanding and practice depend largely on prevailing culture, religious views, and social context. Here in the US, humility is admired, but sometimes the trait is held in tension with individualism. The positive side of humility is that we all recognize the value of modesty, self-awareness, and the ability to put others before oneself. Leaders who show humility are often respected for being approachable and grounded. The challenge in our culture is that true humility can be mistaken for weakness, passivity, or lack of confidence.

The world's view of holiness is more nuanced. Outside of religion, holiness can be seen as acting with "deep moral integrity." At the same time, the Christian tradition veers toward being "set apart" for God and toward living morally pure lives devoted to prayer, love, and service. But let's face it: holiness is more of a divinely inspired event.

One of the main issues we need to wrestle with is finding a holiness overlay to our lives that is different from the world's fixation on "me, myself, and I," which began in the Garden of Eden.

Eve, followed by Adam, rejected God's directive not to eat the forbidden fruit in favor of following their own will, to do what *they* wanted. The result: Eve was misled into believing the fruit would offer knowledge and benefit her, while Adam understood the prohibition but also chose to defy God, likely to be with Eve.

As in the case of almost everything in life, understanding where you are starting from . . . really starting from . . . with self-transparency and all the material issues considered, is critical to getting to one's desired objective.

For the sake of discussion, let's assume that mankind started in a perfect environment with a perfect relationship with our Creator.

No matter how far back you look in human history, people have been pushing their own agenda ever since the dawn of time at significant cost to themselves and their fellow human beings.

Whether one entirely agrees, partially agrees, or doesn't agree doesn't change what is true. The truth is this: we are all born with a "seed of divinity," which points to the idea that within every human being, there is something of God, a spark or a capacity that connects us to the divine. Consider this verse from Genesis:

> So God created man in his own image,
> in the image of God he created him;
> male and female he created them.
>
> —Genesis 1:27 (ESV)

Just as we were born in the image of God, or "Imago Dei" in Latin, we are also born with the seed of sin. We are stained because of the choice Adam and Eve made. They rebelled against God's one rule in the Garden. The result: the sin of the MMI syndrome reared its ugly head in the Garden.

And even if you only partially agree or don't agree, at any point in history—including today—the battle between good and evil and between sin and divinity is as ever-present today as it has ever been.

Thus, the case can be made that the seed of MMI has long been in our hearts, but those who turn to Jesus with humility can begin the long, yet eternally worthwhile, walk toward holiness by following Him. That walk is called the "straight and narrow path" (often phrased as "the narrow gate" and "the hard way" in Matthew 7:13-14, NIV), when Jesus preached the Sermon on the Mount:

> "Enter through the narrow gate. For wide is the gate and broad is the road that leads to destruction, and many enter through it. But small is the gate and narrow the road that leads to life, and only a few find it."

Is there a way to stay on this straight and narrow path as represented in this Scripture?

God's Word often emphasizes the importance of the heart as the source of our actions, thoughts, and how we live out our faith. The heart is the wellspring of life and the seat of our desires, motivations, and affection, which naturally tend to focus inward on self-preservation, self-promotion, and self-gratification. No wonder the attitude of MMI can capture a heart. Jeremiah 17:9 (NIV) reminds us:

> The heart is deceitful above all things
>   and beyond cure.
> Who can understand it?

Yet the Bible also tells us humility and the heart go hand in hand:

> What does the Lord require of you? To act justly, love mercy, and walk humbly with your God.
>
> —MICAH 6:8 (NIV)

> Do nothing out of selfish ambition or vain conceit. Rather, in humility value others above yourselves.
>
> —PHILIPPIANS 2:3-4 (NIV)

That's not about losing yourself. It's about becoming your most authentic self—loving, but not prideful; bold, but not boastful. Whatever your heart is leaning into is where your mind and body will follow.

Humility tempers the heart by reminding us that we are not the center of the universe, no matter how many likes we have. Sure, our feelings matter, but so do others. A humble heart still feels deeply, but it also listens to others, yields when the time is appropriate, and doesn't demand attention or recognition.

To have heart *and* humility, keep these things in mind:

- Serve others without seeking applause.
- Speak truth with kindness, not arrogance.
- Admit wrongs without losing dignity.
- Be vulnerable without being walked on.

In short, having a humble heart enables us to care, and humility provides us with the wisdom to care rightly. As British author and theologian C.S. Lewis once said, "Do not think less of yourself. Think of yourself less."

Here's another quote that I like from Scottish evangelist Oswald Chambers:

> God writes the new name on those places only in our lives where he has erased pride, self-sufficiency, and self-interest. Some have spots only in the new locations, like spiritual measles.

As my good friend and my former pastor Mark Foreman once said, "The degree of revelation will be directly related to the degree of submission."

My wife, Catherine, and I experienced both humility and God's holiness at a level we had not experienced when our son Michael was in his mid-twenties.

With a large family like ours, there are always many prayers offered up to our Lord. There was a season when my wife was exceedingly concerned about certain family members, including Michael. Michael is a gifted creative and has worked with people from different walks of life in the music and art world. This period of time kept her on her knees at a new level she had not yet experienced.

She expressed all her concerns in her prayers, but, like most of us, she continued to carry those worries in her heart and mind. Catherine wondered if and when God would answer her prayers and what those answers would look like.

One day, God placed on her heart a reminder of all the answered prayers she had over the years for our artist and music creator son. That week, she was prompted to visit the places he had lived and worked, starting with his art and the music studio where he lived. When she laid her hands on the building and thanked God, she felt the Lord's presence intimately and tenderly. Then she heard Him say to her as clear as day: *I will answer you in My time, according to My will, and much more abundantly than you can ever imagine.*

She proceeded to each location for the next few days, and He continued to flood her with reminders of the prayers He had answered. It was evident at each location that God was comforting my wife and that she had nothing to fear. He called her to continue trusting in His sovereignty and faithfulness.

On the fifth day of that week, Catherine and I decided to go up north to our vacation home on the Central Coast. We called Michael and invited him to join us. We had low hopes that he could come

We no longer own our vacation home north of Santa Barbara and Point Conception primarily because traffic getting through the Los Angeles area became unbearable, sometimes turning a five-hour trip into seven or eight hours. But the beautiful view we had from this gorgeous home is etched in our minds forever . . . thank you, God

since we had phoned him at the last minute, but to our pleasant surprise, he told us he would meet us there the next day.

When Michael arrived at the house, we hopped into our Toyota Land Cruiser and made our way down to the beach. When we reached the coastline, we were struck by the beauty of the day and the glorious Pacific Ocean, which we all treasured over the years.

We parked the vehicle close to our usual location. That day, the beach was covered with so many abalone shells that it was as though they had rained down from heaven.

"Let's pick some up and take them home," Catherine said, which sounded like a great idea. We had to walk carefully so that we wouldn't step on the incredible number of shells that nearly blanketed the beach. Michael grabbed a 45-gallon trash bag from the back of the Land Cruiser and began picking up as many shells as the bag could hold.

I watched Catherine, and she seemed pensive and far away in thought as we walked along the sandy coastline. We'd been walking on that beach for seventeen years and had never seen anything but a few abalone shells here and there—and those shells were usually partially broken and otherwise blemished. On this day, however, most of the oval-shaped shells were fully intact, and the interiors shimmered in rainbow colors—blues, greens, pinks, purples, and silvers. After we collected about fifty perfect shells, Catherine stopped to explain to Michael and me something she had been doing for seventeen years.

Look at all those amazing abalone shells that Catherine and our son Michael collected on that memorable afternoon! Hundreds had washed up on the shoreline with the tide the night before. God knew what was needed that very special day.

"All these years, when we would come up here and walk on the beach, I'd pray for you and our entire family. I would walk miles and pray and ask God to let me find a perfect abalone shell that I could bring home to you, Michael."

"Why was that, Mom?" our son asked.

"Because I wanted the shell to remind you that I am always thinking about you and praying for you," Catherine replied, "and to be a visual reminder of those prayers, but many times, there were very few shells to pick from. Today, there is an overabundance of perfect shells. And you are here with us."

We remained silent for a short while. I know for me, I felt like I was standing in the presence of a true miracle—a miracle that would have been washed away that night at high tide when all those abalone shells would have been swept back into the ocean. Instead, hundreds of these beautiful shells were waiting for us on the beach on that specific day and at that particular time—a tangible representation of God's love, faithfulness, and holiness, of His omnipresence and His attention to every detail of our lives.

His message to Catherine that day was crystal clear and worth repeating: *Yes, my dear daughter, I will answer your prayers, but they will be in My time and according to My will, and in a way far more abundant than you can ever imagine.* Why God waited for seventeen years to answer that specific prayer in the way He did is something we'll never know, but we do know that He does answer our prayers, in His time, according to His will, and much more abundantly than we can imagine.

He made His promise clear that glorious day on the beach, when the three of us experienced abundant humility and reverential awe in the presence of a Holy God.

Since the concept of holiness relates directly to divinity and godliness, here's another reminder that we humans are called to be holy, as Leviticus 20:26 (ESV) states quite clearly:

> "You shall be holy to me, for I the Lord am holy and have separated you from the peoples, that you should be mine."

So how does that happen, especially since we act like knuckleheads far too often?

There is only one way, and that's by activating the seed of divinity within you.

1 John 3:9 speaks of God's "seed" remaining in those who are born of Him, meaning divine life is implanted in believers, and 2 Peter 1:4 says we may "participate" in His divine nature.

Once that seed is activated, our words, our actions, our successes, and our inevitable failures can be viewed as steps of trust in a broken world.

And just how does this indwelling activation of the Spirit of God in us play out? Consider this Scripture:

> "Instead, whoever wants to become great among you must be your servant, and whoever would be first among you must be your slave—just as the Son of Man did not come to be served, but to serve, and to give his life as a ransom for many."
>
> —Jesus' words in Matthew 20:26-28 (NIV)

The seed of divinity—the spark of almighty God—will not force you to do anything, but the world will do everything it can to distract you from activating that spark into a raging inferno for His honor and glory.

When the seed of divinity is activated, His name is written on your heart.

> "And I will give you a new heart, and I will put a new spirit in you. I take out your stony, stubborn heart and give you a tender, responsive heart. I will put my Spirit in you so that you will follow my decrees and be careful to obey my regulations."
>
> —Ezekiel 36:26-27 (NLT)

That new heart is the beginning of everything good.

In dealing with others and maintaining the humility and holiness that we are called to, our desire should always be to offer a Christ-centered response. That's humility in action, recognizing that we don't have all the answers but need to seek Him because He does.

We need to ask ourselves at every turn and every decision, "What did Jesus do?" By His sinless life, He has already given us every example we need for how to conduct ourselves in all human relationships. Those examples are right in the Bible for all to read and reflect on.

This is the right path to holiness. Holiness is called the will of God because it reflects the merging of both His character and His purpose for people. I've already mentioned that God's nature is holy, but holiness also restores our relationship with Him and shapes our character.

A final thought: holiness prepares us for eternity. Ultimately, God wills holiness because He intends His people to dwell with Him forever. Heaven is a holy place, and holiness is what prepares the heart to live in God's presence:

> Nothing evil will be allowed to enter, nor anyone who practices shameful idolatry and dishonesty—but only those whose names are written in the Lamb's Book of Life.
>
> —Revelation 21:27 (NLT)

And holiness isn't something you do. You don't put on holiness. Holiness is something that is done *to* you and transforms you.

Consider this Scripture from the apostle Peter:

> For this is the will of God, that by doing good you should put to silence the ignorance of foolish people.
>
> —1 PETER 2:15 (ESV)

A cover on *Surfer* magazine years ago showed the hairiest but most perfect fifteen-foot wave any surfer could dream of after drifting off to sleep. The photo depicted a surfer in the perfect position for take-off but pulling back at the last moment, obviously afraid to drop in to such a massive wall of water.

I'll never forget what the caption said: "You don't know if you don't go."

The same thing could be said for everyone who's paddled out in the game of life. Will you drop in or hang back in the lineup? Will you take a risk to experience the most exhilarating ride of your life? Or will you sit on your board, unwilling to engage the crisp, clean sets that God provides and allow the world to give you a fake meaning for life?

Jesus is inviting you to paddle out and paddle in today. He won't force you to drop in. That's your choice. But if you paddle with faith, knowing that the ride might get bumpy and you might even wipe out, He will be there to steady you, and He will be there if you end up getting worked by the wave.

Will it get scary to take on massive waves and trust Him no matter what? At times, yes. Will you feel like you're over your head? Will the rides be challenging? The answer to all these questions is yes, at times.

But if you're willing to trust Him in everything you do, you will significantly reduce your regrets and live a life of readiness. I'm confident that when we someday reflect on how we followed Him and His lead—whether a day or years from now—we will realize how His perfect holiness has seeped into little imperfect you and me. I predict that we'll feel so incredibly grateful looking in the rearview mirror for what He accomplished through us, and we will fall even more in love with Him.

Jesus said:

> "And I, when I am lifted up from the earth, will draw all people to myself."
>
> —JOHN 12:32 (NIV).

By the Cross, He has allowed all men and women to come to Him. And by the power of the Holy Spirit, He activates the seed of divinity within us all. We, too, can lift others up and out of the muck of life that can bog us down more often than we'd like. Don't forget that He draws people to Him through us.

This week, stay humble, recognize you were created to be set apart, be holy, and look for ways to unify yourself with the One who made you and allow Him to work through you.

Praise be the Man on the Middle Cross![1]

1 I invite you to spend around four minutes watching Scottish-born pastor Alistair Begg's sermon excerpt on YouTube. Use these search words: Alistair Begg and "The Man on the Middle Cross."

10

Are You Ready to Serve?

The generous will prosper;
those who refresh others will
themselves be refreshed.

—Proverbs 11:25 (NLT)

At its core, the powerful question—"Are you ready to serve?"—is an invitation to examine your heart, your priorities, and your willingness to give yourself to something greater than your own comfort.

For those of us who are followers of Christ, the words "Are you ready to serve?" are asking whether you are prepared to lay aside your self-interests and make yourself available to God's call to serve others in love. Serving is less about ability and more about availability—a challenge to look at your readiness to act with kindness, responsibility, and selflessness in everyday life.

So, what does it mean to serve others, which is another way of saying being in service with others?

Merriam-Webster defines service as "the occupation or

function of serving, the work performed by one that serves, contribution to the welfare of others, and a helpful act or labor that does not produce a tangible commodity."

Those are sound definitions: most people believe serving means volunteering at a soup kitchen or becoming a waiter or waitress, taking people's orders, and carrying meals from the restaurant kitchen to the table. I believe "serving" means putting others' needs above your own, whether in family, friendships, or community. Furthermore, adopting a service-oriented attitude—seeking ways to serve others rather than prioritizing our own needs and desires—is the best approach. Realizing that life feels more meaningful when filled with service to others is critical.

I love these quotes on serving others:

> "Service is the rent you pay for room on this earth."
>
> —Shirley Chisholm, the first black woman elected to the United States Congress

> "There is no greater satisfaction for a just and well-meaning person than the knowledge that he or she has devoted their best energies to the service of a good cause."
>
> —Albert Einstein, German-born physicist who lived from 1879 to 1955

> "The best servant does his work unseen."
>
> —Oliver Wendell Holmes Sr., American physician and poet who lived from 1809 to 1894

> "The man who is himself at ease can best attend to the distress of others."
>
> —Adam Smith, 18th-century economist and philosopher

> "Twenty years from now, you will be more disappointed by the things you didn't do than by the things you did."
>
> —MARK TWAIN, American writer and humorist who lived from 1835 to 1910.

> "If living a life of true meaning is important to you, then serving others has to be an essential component."
>
> —JAY WENTZ, author of *Are You Ready?*

Yes, I'm having some fun slipping myself in among the galaxy of celebrity voices on the topic of service. Still, everyone pales in wisdom and insight to our Lord Jesus Christ, who emphasized that His purpose was to serve others, not to be served:

> "You know that the rulers in this world lord it over their people, and officials flaunt their authority over those under them. But among you it will be different. Whoever wants to be a leader among you must be your servant, and whoever wants to be first among you must become your slave. For even the Son of Man came not to be served but to serve others and to give his life as a ransom for many."
>
> —MATTHEW 20:25-28 (NLT)

Furthermore, Jesus said this about serving others:

> "If you have two shirts, give one to the poor. If you have food, share it with those who are hungry."
>
> —LUKE 3:11 (NLT)

The apostle Paul wrote that bearing one another's burdens fulfills the law of Christ (Galatians 6:2). Earlier in his letter to the Galatians, he encouraged humble service to others in love:

> For you have been called to live in freedom, my brothers and sisters. But don't use your freedom to satisfy your sinful nature. Instead, use your freedom to serve one another in love.
>
> —GALATIANS 5:13 (NLT)

And finally, the apostle Peter urges believers to use their spiritual gifts to serve one another as good stewards of God's grace:

> God has given each of you a gift from his great variety of spiritual gifts. Use them well to serve one another.
>
> —1 PETER 4:10 (NLT)

We become a servant when another's well-being is as important or more important than our own, and we act on it.

As previously discussed, each of us is born with the seed of Divinity and the seed of sin. The seed of sin includes the "me, myself, and I" syndrome in our DNA, so it takes a lot to overcome our natural impulse to look out for No. 1. Unfortunately, the MMI syndrome pretty much dominates the world's landscape of who will be served, how they should be served, and why they should be served.

For most people, service is an afterthought and often self-serving (code for "What's in it for me?"). If we serve others, it's because we want something in return. *I'll scratch your back, and you scratch mine.*

Back when Catherine and I were recently married, we moved from our first home into a new neighborhood. I had started working with an upstart nonprofit organization that helped the homeless in downtown San Diego. Well, that group had a truck that looked like the old jalopy Jed Clampett drove in the 1960s sitcom, *The Beverly Hillbillies.*

I thought it would be a good idea to hire a couple of the homeless to help us move. A win-win for both sides, right? The homeless workers would earn a day's wage and get back into the habit of making some money, and I would get some help carrying our furniture and heavy boxes during the move.

We worked hard to load that old flat-bed truck, ringed with wooden barriers, with all our stuff. You should have seen us as we barreled down Interstate 5 to our new home. We got quite a few stares of disbelief from other drivers as I sat behind the wheel of that rusty bucket of bolts with two homeless guys perched on the bench seat.

We arrived at our new place and started unloading our stuff. In fact, it took several back-and-forth loads to complete our move, so I really appreciated the guys' help, as Catherine and I couldn't have managed without it. I expressed my appreciation by greasing their palms with some hard-earned cash.

After the last load, I took the guys back to downtown San Diego and returned to our new place, where Catherine and I began the long, tedious process of unpacking. We were hanging up clothes and emptying boxes of clothes when I noticed something amiss.

"Have you seen my favorite pair of boots and my cowboy belt buckle?" I asked. I loved wearing my wannabe cowboy boots and "fashion-statement" cowboy belt buckle now and then.

"Don't worry, honey," she replied. "They'll show up." The fact is, she never liked the boots or the buckle.

Well, my boots and buckle didn't show up. I couldn't find them anywhere.

I shrugged off the development, figuring my old "favs" got lost in the move or we'd find them when we finished unpacking the remaining boxes. But a week later, I was working at the nonprofit when I looked up and noticed one of the homeless men who helped us move was wearing my boots and belt buckle!

Of course, I didn't have the heart to ask for items back. I figured he needed them more than I did. But in the back of my mind, I felt like this was a good way to serve my fellow man—by not making a big deal out of a pair of missing cowboy boots and oversized belt buckle.

Then this Scripture came to mind:

> "The Lord gave, and the Lord has taken away. Blessed be the name of the Lord."
>
> —Job 1:21 (NASB)

Yes, I could turn this into an opportunity to praise the Lord, which I was pleased to do.

I was also reminded of a scene from the Disney movie *Finding Nemo,* in which seagulls flew around and around, constantly fighting over scraps of food, repeating the words, "Mine, mine, mine" with each swoop to the ground. I didn't want to be that way. I never want my possessions to own me. It's all just stuff, right?

I'm glad I didn't raise a fuss about the missing boots and belt buckle. More than thirty years later, Catherine and I are still chuckling about this interaction—and I'm grateful for the lesson I learned.

Sometimes the best opportunities to serve come through the actions of others.

I believe my attitude toward serving others was nurtured by the way I was raised. Every Christmas and Easter, my father would dress up as Santa Claus or the Easter Bunny and take my siblings and me with him to visit the elderly in nursing homes and sick children in hospitals, bringing them presents.

I thought it was pretty funny seeing my string-bean six-foot, three-inch father donning an ill-fitting Santa Claus suit or silly wabbit suit, as did the elderly folks and children we visited. Sure, he looked ridiculous, but what Dad instilled in me at a very young age was that there was something very special about stepping out and stepping up for others.

Here's a more spiritual way of looking at why serving others is a good thing to do:

1. **Serving gives us a chance to live out love.** Serving others is a way of embodying God's love—putting compassion, mercy, and kindness into action rather than keeping them as mere ideas or feelings.
2. **Serving allows us to follow God's example.** Scripture often portrays God as one who cares for the poor, heals the brokenhearted, and lifts the lowly. When we serve, we imitate His character. It's a way of reflecting the divine image placed within us.
3. **Serving reminds us of the importance of humility and transformation and requires us to step down from pride and self-interest.** In humbling ourselves, our hearts are reshaped. Service becomes not only a blessing to others but also a tool for our own spiritual growth.

4. **Spiritually, service is often described as being "the hands and feet" of a higher calling.** We become instruments of peace, healing, and provision—meeting needs in tangible ways that point back to God's care.
5. **Serving has eternal value.** While personal achievements may fade, acts of service ripple into eternity. Serving aligns us with God's kingdom work, which carries lasting weight and meaning beyond this life.
6. **Serving can be looked at as a sacred exchange.** When we serve, we often find that we receive as much as we give—peace, joy, deeper faith, and a clearer sense of God's presence. Service becomes a form of worship, a sacred act that blesses both giver and receiver.

When we serve others, we step into the heart of God's will. Isn't that cool? Service is not just a task or duty—it's a sacred expression of love. Every time we lend a hand, speak a kind word, or give of ourselves, we mirror the compassion of Christ, who came not to be served but to serve.

In moments of service, something holy takes place. The walls of pride begin to crumble, and humility has room to grow. Holiness and humility—what I discussed in my last chapter. When we meld these two characteristics, we start to see people as God sees them—beloved, worthy, and precious in His sight. The act of helping another becomes more than a good deed; it becomes an act of worship, a quiet offering laid at God's feet.

Often, when we serve, we think we're giving to others. Yet in the mystery of God's design, we will find ourselves receiving joy that cannot be measured, a peace that steadies the soul, and a deeper awareness of God's presence moving through us. Service becomes a channel of grace, reminding us that in God's kingdom, giving and receiving are intertwined.

And so, to serve others is to walk in step with Christ. In serving, we discover our truest self and our truest calling: to love as we have first been loved (1 John 4:19).

We need to be careful, though, about "getting over our skis" in our desire to serve God until we've spent time in His Word getting to know Him better:

> We can slander God by our very eagerness to serve Him without knowing Him.
>
> —OSWALD CHAMBERS, author of *My Utmost for the Highest*

God is the source of all righteousness, which is defined as right being, right thinking, and right doing. By taking the time to sit with Him first, we make it much more likely that our own idea of "righteousness" doesn't replace His and that we don't get ahead of God, ourselves, or others. I like this quote from Major W. Ian Thomas, British evangelist and author of *The Indwelling Life of Christ:*

> So long as Christians are busy doing for God what is best in their eyes, they will never enter into His rest and the true inheritance that is theirs to enjoy now. Righteousness is doing what is right in God's eyes.

True service involves a desire to improve someone else's life. However, most of the world is too busy improving their own lives and focusing on their own needs. But when we serve others, we're also making time to listen to one another. Listening builds the Kingdom—and helps us get to know each other better. Many people fail to get along because they don't know the other person or what makes them tick. The ramifications are seen on every news outlet every day, regardless of your political persuasion. Check out this quote from civil rights activist Martin Luther King Jr. in a speech he delivered at Cornell College in Mount Vernon, Iowa, in 1962:

> "People fail to get along [and perhaps avoid serving others] because they fear each other; they fear each other because they don't know each other; they don't know each other because they have not communicated with each other."

Don't roll over the words of another. Listen with an open heart, a skill that requires patience and focus. Many good things slip by us without proper reflection because we are moving so fast to achieve something for ourselves. The process of active listening is a skill requiring patience and focus.

While the world often tells us to "chase our dreams," as if that's our highest calling, life is bigger than our personal ambitions, especially when it involves striving to follow Jesus.

Sure, dreams are good, especially in the way they give us direction, energy, and something to shoot for. But life also calls us to things that don't always line up with our hopes and plans—things like serving others, loving well, walking through hardships with integrity, cultivating gratitude, and living in harmony with God's purposes.

Scripture reminds us that life is more than the pursuit of self:

> For in him we live and move and have our being.
>
> —Acts 17:28 (NIV)

True love and true living are discovered in surrender: in laying our dreams at the feet of the One who brought us into this world and gave us breath. When we do, we find that God's purposes are always broader, deeper, and richer than anything we could have imagined for ourselves. When we allow the Son of God to be formed in and revealed through us, we can serve Him out of pure devotion and in ways we were uniquely designed for.

To serve others, to walk humbly, to love sacrificially—these are callings that outshine personal ambition. And in those hidden moments of obedience, when no spotlight shines, we discover the joy of being caught up in and being an active participant in God's greater story.

We've been given our assignment very clearly by Jesus. We are to steward our gifts for the sake of others—and then serve others with those gifts. We don't need to desire and aspire to be the very best person we can be unless it's for His glory and not ours.

We cannot fake the disposition of Jesus. It's either in us or it's not.

Since God has entrusted us with responsibility for His possessions and gifts, which include time, talents, and treasures, we must manage these gifts faithfully, even in the little things. As that great philosopher Winnie the Pooh once said, "Sometimes the smallest things take up the most room in your heart."

What most people see of us is our responses to our life situations. There are very few people with whom we scratch the surface, but we can still create a positive or negative memory for anyone in the shortest amount of time with a simple reaction. When that happens, ask yourself this: *Did I leave the fragrance of Jesus Christ?*

American memoirist and poet Maya Angelou said it well: "People will forget what you said, people will forget what you did, but people will never forget how you made them feel."

I was standing next to the kitchen stove early one morning several years ago when, suddenly, I forgot what I was doing and the thought of a dear friend came to mind. He had reached out the day before to tell me he was praying for Catherine when she was going through an issue I've long forgotten.

But what made this exchange compelling was that my dear friend was dealing with a life-threatening cancer at the time, yet he took the time to pray for Catherine and then reach out to tell me that he was praying for her. How selfless and serving was my friend, who lost his life several weeks later to deadly cancer.

You could say that he followed this Scripture right to the end:

> Don't look out only for your own interests, but take an interest in others, too.
>
> —PHILIPPIANS 2:4 (NLT)

Kindness is the most powerful tool in our Christian tool belt. In a world that prizes strength, success, and self-assertion, kindness can often seem insignificant or overlooked. Yet in the way of Christ, kindness is one of the most potent tools we carry because kindness reflects the very heart of God:

> But when the kindness and love of God our Savior appeared, he saved us, not because of righteous things we had done, but because of his mercy. He saved us through the washing of rebirth and renewal by the Holy Spirit, whom he poured out on us generously through Jesus Christ our Savior, so that, having been justified by his grace, we might become heirs having the hope of eternal life.
>
> —TITUS 3:4–7 (NIV)

It is through kindness that God drew us to Himself, not through force or fear. When we extend kindness, we mirror His character, showing others the same grace we ourselves have received.

Kindness disarms hostility. A gentle word softens anger; a patient response silences insult. Kindness transforms ordinary encounters into sacred opportunities, where hearts are open to hear the truth and love. Even the smallest act—an encouraging word, a listening ear, a simple act of help—can ripple outward further than we know.

Unlike talents or achievements, kindness requires no special stage. It can be practiced anywhere, from home to the checkout line, on the street corner, and yes, even on social media. It is always within reach. And when given, it carries eternal weight, for kindness plants seeds of God's kingdom in the soil of everyday life.

Kindness is powerful because it is not of us—it flows through us from Christ. **To put on kindness is to put on Christ Himself (Colossians 3:12).** And in doing so, we wield a tool that can change lives more deeply than argument or accomplishment ever could.

We almost always recognize the moment when kindness is extended to us—or we should. The spark of Divinity recognizes the reciprocal spark directed to it.

A watershed example of selfless servanthood occurred in the

1950s when a missionary named Jim Elliot and several companions were led to bring the gospel to the Ecuadorian jungle. Armed with Bibles, they traveled deep upriver. Even before he had an opportunity to share the gospel with the Huaorani people, Jim Elliott was killed by the natives.

In his diary, Jim Elliott had written these words: **"He is no fool who gives up what he cannot keep to gain what he cannot lose."** This quote suggests that sacrificing temporary things for eternal gain is a wise investment because it prioritizes lasting spiritual rewards over perishable material possessions.

Jim Elliott was ready to serve.

After he and four other missionaries were killed in 1956 by Amazon tribe members, their sacrifice led to the Huaorani people's conversion to Christianity through the courageous ministry of their widows, including Elisabeth Elliot.

Jim Elliot and the other missionaries put their lives on the line to serve people they didn't know because they wanted to share the gospel and the hope of eternal life with Christ.

So, let me ask a personal question: How are you using your time, talents, and treasure to make the world a better place?

It's a question that I often have to ask myself. Keep these thoughts in mind:

- **Time is the most limited resource we have.** Once spent, time can't be recovered. Using time well means serving others, giving undivided attention to loved ones, actively listening, and slowing down long enough to notice people who often feel invisible. It's about having a mindset that prioritizes eternal values—faith, relationships, and love—over distractions that only drain us.
- **Talents are the skills, passions, and experiences**

that God gives us. We can use them to equip others and mentor them so that our skills multiply beyond ourselves.

- **Treasure is more than money.** Treasures are whatever resources we hold in our hands that can bless others. That includes finances, possessions, influence, and opportunities. We can give generously, recognizing that the money we have is not just for our comfort but for kingdom impact.

When we weave these three strands together—time, talents, and treasure—we become co-workers with God in renewing the world. The measure isn't how much we give, but whether we give faithfully with love and joy. None of these three gifts belongs to us; they are entrusted to us as stewards, with the invitation to use them for His glory and the good of others.

The benefits of serving others flow on many levels—spiritual, emotional, relational, and even physical. Serving draws us closer to God because it shifts our focus from self to Savior. Serving others deepens our intimacy with God as we learn to see people through His eyes and love them with His heart.

Serving others shapes our character. You could say that service is God's classroom for humility, patience, and compassion, stretching us beyond comfort and chiseling away our selfishness and pride. **When we give ourselves away, we are transformed into the likeness of Christ.**

Serving brings joy and fulfillment. There's a unique joy in knowing you've lightened somebody's burden. Science even confirms what Scripture teaches—that giving of yourself produces joy, lowers stress, and increases a sense of purpose in life. As Jesus said, "It is more blessed to give than to receive" (Acts 20:35, NIV).

Every act of service, no matter how small, echoes in eternity.

A kind word, a helping hand, and a financial gift are never wasted. God uses them to plant seeds of hope, faith, and love that grow far beyond what we can see or imagine. Serving others makes us real.

In the British children's book, *The Velveteen Rabbit*, author Margery Williams chronicles the story of a stuffed rabbit's desire to become real through the (serving) love of its owner. Here's an excerpt:

> "Real isn't how you are made," said the Skin Horse. "It's the thing that happens to you." When a child loves you for a long, long time, not just to play with but *really* loves you, then you become Real.
>
> "Does it hurt?" asked the Rabbit.
>
> "Sometimes," said the Skin Horse, for he was always truthful. When you are Real, you don't mind being hurt."
>
> "Does it happen all at once, like being wound up," he asked, "or bit by bit?"
>
> "It doesn't happen all at once," said the Skin Horse. "You become. It takes a long time. That's why it doesn't happen often to people who break easily, or have sharp edges, or have to be carefully kept. Generally, by the time you are Real, most of your hair has been loved off, and your eyes drop out, and you get loose in the joints and very shabby. But these things don't matter at all, because once you are Real you can't be ugly, except to people who don't understand."

When we serve others, we help them become Real—I've capitalized the word as Margery Williams did—and in that act of love, we become more Real also.

11

Are You Ready for Perfect Imperfection?

"The closest to perfection a person ever comes is when he fills out a job application form."

—Stanley J. Randall, Canadian businessman and political figure in the 20th century

I've spent a lot of time in *Are You Ready?* talking about the difference between the world's approach and Jesus' approach to some of life's most essential questions of readiness.

Most of us want to improve ourselves, become better people, and find real meaning in our lives, which is a great way to go through life. My point is this: at the end of the day—or more accurately, at the end of our existence—none of these efforts will amount to anything unless we seek first the kingdom of God, as Jesus taught in the Sermon on the Mount:

> "But seek first the kingdom of God and his righteousness, and all these things will be added to you."
>
> —Matthew 6:33 (ESV)

What Jesus said is counter-cultural—even offensive—to our modern mindset, which insists that if you optimize, grind, work hard, and achieve financial success, then life will be perfect. You'll have security, happiness, significance, and provision—everything required for a "perfect" life.

This leads me to a fundamental question: **What is the world's approach to perfection?**

In the world's vocabulary, the words *perfection* and *imperfection* are mutually exclusive. Imperfections are viewed as flaws—evidence of diminished capacity or failed results—while perfection is pursued through accomplishment and acquisition.

The notion of perfection in our culture is celebrated loudly and relentlessly every day. Consider just a few of the things we often chase—sometimes obsessively:

- **The perfect school.** We all know parents who obsess with getting their children into the "perfect" kindergarten, which feeds into the perfect private elementary school, the perfect private high school, and ultimately the perfect Ivy League college.
- **The perfect career.** The perfect job offers high pay, plenty of vacation and "personal" days, endless growth, a healthy work-life balance, and encouraging bosses.
- **The perfect romantic partner.** He or she is the perfect soulmate who's physically attractive, reads your mind, thinks like you, and inspires others to say, "That's a match made in heaven."
- **The perfect child or perfect children.** The perfect baby sleeps through the night right after birth. The perfect toddler never throws a

tantrum in public. Perfect kids are straight-A students and star athletes.

- **The perfect body.** I'm talking about a fixation on special diets, exercise plans, and surgical procedures like breast augmentation, liposuction, and tummy tucks. And don't forget about Botox injections. We're in a continual quest to look our best—to look perfect.

And last but not least:

- **The perfect church.** The worship music is great, the preaching is spot-on, the elders and pastors are above reproach in every possible way, and there's perfect unity throughout the congregation.

The trouble is, there's no perfect church. We all carry baggage, blind spots, and remaining sin. As the old saying goes, "The perfect church ceases to be perfect the moment any of us walks in the door."

At day's end, the world does not offer *perfect imperfection*. Instead, it leaves us either lamenting our flaws or endlessly grasping for things that promise fulfillment but ultimately leave us empty.

The world claims to promote contentment, but what it really cultivates is a restless spirit—a perpetual sense of lack. Nothing good grows in the soil of "never enough," and its toxicity is everywhere.

But so is the ultimate alternative—Jesus.

We were created for relationship with God, and we will be restless until we rest in Him.

So, is perfection achievable in this life?

From a Christian perspective, the answer is simple: **No, not at all:**

> Nowhere in the Bible is there any support for the promise of sinless perfection except on that wonderful day when we see the Lord Jesus Christ face to face. Then indeed, "we shall be like Him for we shall see Him as he is" (1 John 3:2).
>
> —MAJOR IAN W. THOMAS, author of *The Indwelling Life of Christ*

Nothing and no one on this Earth is perfect or ever will be. Only God is perfect.

We can see His perfect mind in how He created this incredibly detailed universe that works *perfectly in countless ways*:

- The Earth spins at one thousand miles per hour, yet we don't feel it because the atmosphere moves with us in smooth, constant motion. That speed produces a twenty-four-hour day. Any faster or slower would mean significant—potentially catastrophic changes—in climate, sea levels, and geology. The Earth's current rotation speed is a delicate balance that has allowed life to flourish.
- The surface of the Sun burns at roughly ten thousand degrees Fahrenheit. Yet the Earth orbits at just the right distance—93 million miles—within the Sun's "habitable zone," where the amount of sunlight we receive gives us an average temperature of around 59 degrees—not too hot, not too cold. Perfect for liquid water and life as we know it.

- Consider the incredible miracle of life created in a woman's womb: millions of cells multiplying daily for nine months from a simple union of just the sperm and the egg. Two to three weeks after conception, the brain is developing 250,000 neurons per minute. A newborn baby arrives with roughly fifty million neurological connections, which increase by one million new connections per second.

Seems like perfection in design from the Designer behind it all!

So here's the deal: the world doesn't need a "perfect" version of you. Sure, excellence is worth pursuing in any task or career, but perfection is unattainable. Any attempt to live a worldly-perfect life—or to redeem yourself—will ultimately rob you of real meaning and a lasting legacy.

Consider a few favorite quotations of mine:

> "Perfection consists of one thing only: doing the will of God."
>
> —St. Vincent de Paul, a Catholic saint who dedicated himself to serving the poor and lived from 1581 to 1660

> "A work is perfectly finished only when nothing can be added to it, and nothing's taken away."
>
> —Joseph Joubert, French moralist who lived from 1754 to 1824

> "The true perfection of a man lies not in what a man has but in what a man is."
>
> —Oscar Wilde, Irish poet and playwright who lived from 1854 to 1900

The Christian hope rests in this truth: God sees us perfect in Christ now, and Christ will complete His perfect work in us when He returns.

Those who chase the "perfect life" through self-redemptive efforts will discover some of the most common, brutal side effects of self-perfectionism, such as:

- **Chronic burnout and exhaustion.** Without the freedom to say, "That's good enough," we drain our energy stores and risk shutting down completely.
- **Toxic relationships.** Expecting perfection from your spouse, your kids, your friends, or your work life guarantees frustration and disappointment.
- **Getting caught up in the comparison game.** We can see the quest for perfection on social media, where people only show the world the "perfect" side of themselves: exotic vacations abroad, amazing entrees at fancy restaurants, and glorious sunsets, but we all intuitively know the truth side of a "Photoshopped" life.

Perfectionism doesn't make us excellent—it makes us fragile, isolated, and perpetually dissatisfied. We are imperfect creatures because of the seed of sin within us.

So, what is imperfection?

Human imperfection is not merely a psychological reality—it is a theological truth woven into the very fabric of Scripture.

Though we're created in God's image, we are marked by weakness, limitation, and moral frailty. Our imperfections are not accidents of creation; they remind us of our dependence on God and our need for His grace.

Here are some key truths to remember:

1. **Imperfection reveals our need for God.** From the moment sin entered the world, human beings became prone to wandering, failing, and falling short. Scripture declares, "For all have sinned and fall short of the glory of God" (Romans 3:23). Our imperfections expose the gap between God's holiness and our humanity, drawing our hearts toward repentance and reliance.
2. **Imperfection is where God's strength fully meets our weaknesses.** The apostle Paul learned that weakness was not something to hide but something God could redeem and use. The Lord told him, "My grace is sufficient for you, for my power is made perfect in weakness" (2 Corinthians 12:9, ESV).
3. **Imperfection reminds us that we are still being formed.** We are works in progress, shaped over our lifetime by the Holy Spirit. Paul describes this ongoing transformation:

> And we all, who with unveiled faces contemplate the Lord's glory, are being transformed into his image with ever-increasing glory, which comes from the Lord, who is the Spirit.
>
> —2 Corinthians 3:18 (NIV)

Human imperfection is not a flaw God overlooked—it is a reminder of His grace, an invitation to humility, and a pathway to spiritual growth. Our weaknesses point to the One who is infinitely strong. Our failures highlight the Savior who reconciles us to the Father. And our incompleteness keeps us longing for the day when Christ will make all things new.

God created us perfectly when He made us in His own image and likeness (Genesis 1:26-27). We are not accidents or simply an upgrade from animals. We carry within us an immortal soul and the seed of Divinity that can reason, choose freely, create beauty, and say "I love You" back to God. How cool is that?

At the same time, because of Adam and Eve's sin in the Garden, we have bodies that age, ache, and die—but they will rise again immortal and flawless. That sounds like perfection to me!

Until that moment when we draw our last breath—and that day will inevitably arrive—we can view ourselves as the masterpieces in God's eyes, regardless of our shortcomings. We can humbly and gratefully stand before the God who made us and say:

> I praise you, for I'm fearfully and wonderfully made.
> Wonderful are your works;
> my soul knows it very well.
>
> —Psalm 139:14 (ESV)

> For we are his workmanship, created in Christ Jesus for good works, which God prepared beforehand, that we should walk in them.
>
> —Ephesians 2:10 (ESV)

One of the great paradoxes of the Christian life is this: **we are undeniably imperfect, yet undeniably God's workmanship.** Both realities stand side by side in Scripture, not as contradictions but as complementary truths that exhibit the heart of God.

The world may judge us harshly, but the only verdict that matters is "not guilty" pronounced over you if Jesus is your Lord. If so, God sees you as perfect in His Son.

In Matthew 5:48 (ESV), Jesus tells us, "You therefore must be perfect, as your heavenly Father is perfect." What might seem to be a contradiction in Romans 3:10 (ESV)—"None is righteous, no, not one"—is not a contrary statement because Jesus, by His perfect work on the Cross, melded two opposing dynamics.

Our failures, our mistakes, our "imperfections" if you will, do not define us and should not determine who we are. Sure, we will screw up along the way, but when we trust in Jesus, we are always viewed as perfect in God's eyes. (Yes, an exhale of gratitude is appropriate here.)

This all means God does not wait for perfection before He begins His work in us. He starts with the clay (that would be you and me) as He finds it—cracked, uneven, resistant—and shapes it patiently into what He intended us to be all along. **Our imperfections do not disqualify us from His purposes; instead, they become the very canvas upon which His grace is displayed.**

Furthermore, God is not surprised by our imperfections; He works through them. The apostle Paul reinforces this in Philippians 2:13 (ESV):

> For it is God who works in you, both to will and to work for his good pleasure.

That means our imperfections—past, present, and future—cannot derail His purposes. He uses ordinary, imperfect people to carry out extraordinary kingdom work.

Remember:

Moses stuttered.

David stumbled.

Peter denied Christ.

Paul called himself the "chief of sinners."

Yet God's workmanship shone through them all.

The Holy Spirit is the divine artisan shaping Christ's image within us day by day. As Paul writes, "Our inner self is being renewed day by day" (2 Corinthians 4:16, ESV) and "conformed to the image of His Son" (Romans 8:29, ESV).

This sanctifying process is God's answer to our imperfection: He does not erase it instantly; He redeems us immediately and perfects us gradually:

> "There is no heaven with a little corner of hell in it. God is determined to make you pure and holy and right. He will not allow you to escape for one moment from the scrutiny of the Holy Spirit."
>
> —Oswald Chambers from his book, *My Utmost for His Highest*

The beauty of the gospel is not that God uses perfect people—it is that He uses imperfect ones to reveal His perfect love. Our shortcomings can showcase His mercy. Our wounds can become testimonies of healing. Our limitations can demonstrate His power. In this way, imperfections are not obstacles to God's workmanship—they are the very medium He uses for His glory.

So, while we will never reach a point on planet Earth where all our decisions are correct, because Jesus lives in us, these little imperfect vessels of clay—you and me—can transmit perfect truth even before we meet Him on the other side, where we will see Him and be like Him . . . as in perfectly perfect. How cool will that be?

Jesus Christ is God's own message of perfect love . . . while the Christian religion is man's imperfect interpretation of God's perfect message.

My wife and I live in a historic home built in 1935. Our residence is an excellent example of a pre-World War II California Ranch with American Colonial detailing. Friends and neighbors tell us that our place is charming—and it is. The thing about old homes, though, is that there's always something that needs to be done to keep them in good repair.

Because we feel that our home is "perfect" for us, we're also aware that imperfections come with age and must be addressed sooner or later. That's why we like to say that our "Wonderland"— our nickname for our home—is an example of "perfect imperfection."

Every one of us who believes in and trusts in Jesus is an example of "perfect imperfection" as well. Is it possible that we can view our lives as perfectly imperfect? Why not?

Each day, we experience beautiful "perfect imperfections" that make life on Earth feel human, poignant, and alive. I'll start with sunsets, which last only a few minutes and are imperfect in their brevity. Yet their impermanence is precisely what makes them breathtaking. If a sunset lasted all day, we'd never notice.

The human memory—mine included—fades and becomes less reliable as we age. Yet there's a softness within our minds that turns events into stories, nostalgia, and meaning. Our bodies bear scars and stretch marks—imperfections, for sure—but they also say, "I grew," "I healed," or "I survived." Wrinkles, slower steps, and forgetting names—every mark of aging should remind us that we've been here long enough to matter, and that **we're leaving a legacy of one kind or another.**

Although God created us perfectly, we are not *perfectly* finished, like a statue locked in marble. Instead, we are perfectly *begun*. Every tear you've cried, every time you've fallen and gotten back up, every setback in your life and career—those are not imperfections. Those are brushstrokes from the Artist who is still at work in you, preparing you for a glory that you cannot yet imagine.

Imperfection has a way of drawing us toward community. The Bible never expects believers to walk alone. Our imperfections make us interdependent, designed to encourage, correct, forgive, and support one another. The apostle Paul writes:

> Bear one another's burdens, and so fulfill the law of Christ.
>
> —Galatians 6:2 (ESV)

Where we are weak, others may be strong; where we falter, others uphold us. Imperfection becomes the soil in which love grows. Leading with love is rarely misunderstood.

When the speed of change doesn't conveniently match a burst of clarity about the way things ought to be, be patient—with yourself and with others. Rome was not built in a day. Situations take time to wind up and take time to wind down. What is of paramount importance is leaning your heart toward True North. Life is about steps . . . a whole lot of them.

God knows we are imperfect, and yet we are being shaped by Christ to accomplish the good works He prepared for us long before we learned how to walk in them. This means our imperfections—past, present, and future—cannot derail His purposes. They become tools in God's hands, producing humility, compassion, dependence, and obedience—qualities essential for the works He has prepared.

Oswald Chambers once said:

> You don't become clean little by little. You become white as snow the moment you willfully choose to interact with the great mystery of the Redemption and call on Jesus as your Savior . . . from that point forward, it is by your obedience that revelations come to you and your increasing closeness to and knowledge of the Way becomes real.

Obedience doesn't make us cleaner—but it makes us smarter and allows us to move ever closer to our perfected self. Jesus said:

> "If you love me, you will keep my commandments."
>
> —John 14:15 (ESV)

I'll close with a vivid illustration of our "imperfect perfection," the Christian paradox that God works through flawed people to reveal His grace, presence, humor, and protection.

A few years ago, I took my son-in-law, Scott Schreckengaust, and grandson, John, on an African safari. While traveling through the savannah, our vehicle became stuck in deep sand. The guides told us we would have to get out of the Land Rover and jump into another four-wheel-drive vehicle parked about thirty yards away.

I was halfway there when I realized I had left an expensive Patagonia sweatshirt in the stuck vehicle. I raced back to retrieve it and had the prized sweatshirt in my hand when I heard loud crashing-and-crunching sounds coming from trees behind me.

"Run, Papa Jay, run!" my grandson yelled.

When I looked in the direction of the loud noise, I saw an enormous bull elephant tumbling through the bush—and it was headed straight for me.

Woah!

Fortunately, I didn't have to drop my prized sweatshirt as I sprinted to the vehicle and hopped in just in the nick of time.

This safari moment captures the very essence of our "imperfect perfection" as human beings. On the surface, my story is almost humorous: a grown man leaves the safety of a Land Rover to dash—not for a person, not for a passport, but for a Patagonia sweatshirt.

What I did was such a human thing to do. We cling to what is familiar, valuable, or comforting, even when wisdom might say, "Not a good idea, Jay. You're in an African jungle!" My very human imperfection set the stage for the drama that followed.

But in God's economy, our imperfections don't cancel His care. In fact, they often become the backdrop for His protection and grace to shine more clearly. My moment of distraction—my dash back to the stuck Land Rover—wasn't a perfect decision. Yet God was still there. He preserved me in the midst of my misjudgment, shielding me from a charging bull elephant I never saw coming until it was nearly upon me.

Here's how I break down my "perfect imperfection":

- I made a flawed decision, yet a flawless God protected me.
- Out of my human weakness, I was held within divine strength.
- In a moment of forgetfulness, that moment became unforgettable because of God's mercy.

My grandson's shout—"Run, Papa Jay, run!"—embodies

another truth of our imperfect perfection: God often uses others, even children, to alert us, protect us, and call us back to safety. We were never designed to navigate life alone. Imperfection draws us into community; weakness opens us to help.

Going on an African safari with my son-in-law, Scott Schreckenguast, and my grandson, John, was epic—although we got a little too up close and personal with some animals we saw in the wild.

And finally, my African safari story reminds us that God does not wait for us to be perfect before He acts on our behalf. He does not require flawless judgment, flawless courage, or flawless behavior. He simply meets us where we are—sweatshirt in hand, dust on our shoes, hearts pounding—and delivers us in His timing.

Remember:

- We are imperfect . . . yet we are His workmanship (Ephesians 2:10).
- We make questionable decisions . . . yet He rescues, teaches, and shapes us through them.
- We stumble into danger . . . yet His grace runs faster than any bull elephant crashing through the trees.

At the end of the day, your life story is not just an adventure tale. You are a living parable of the God who continually works His perfect purposes through imperfect people—turning ordinary human moments into extraordinary testimonies of His protection and love.

Recognizing this indelible truth will change your life forever.

12

Are You Ready for Your Final Breath?

A Concluding Thought

"The two most important days of your life are the day you are born, and the day you find out why."

—Mark Twain, humorist and novelist (1836-1910)

In our journey together, we have walked through some of the most common readiness issues that every human being faces.

I've asked you if you're ready to see yourself as Jesus sees you. I've asked if you're ready to slow down and smell the roses, ready to deal with adversity in your life, and ready to serve others. I've asked if you're ready to consider Jesus' words and actions as a different and far better way to live.

I hope I've given good information along the way because good information makes for good decisions. Far better still is the Good News in God's Word—the best information ever written. I believe all the words in the Bible are Jesus' words because it's His book. He is the Word of God (John 1:1), and He divinely inspired all writers in the Bible to write every word:

> All Scripture is breathed out by God and profitable for teaching, for reproof, for correction, and for training in righteousness . . .
>
> – 2 Timothy 3:16 (ESV)

It is in Jesus that all knowledge and wisdom are found:

> . . . that their hearts may be encouraged, being knit together in love, to reach all the riches of full assurance of understanding and the knowledge of God's mystery, which is Christ, in whom are hidden all the treasures of wisdom and knowledge.
>
> –Colossians 2:2-3 (ESV)

God's Word is "truth north"—the absolute, eternal, and reliable guide for life. Just as navigators seek out a fixed, unchanging direction toward the geographic North Pole—known as "true north"—Jesus is the fixed point that never changes, even as the world shifts (Hebrews 13:8). Following Him keeps you on the correct path to eternal life, righteousness, and fulfilment.

When it comes to living a life of true meaning, you don't want to rely on a compass pointing to "magnetic north," which is influenced by the Earth's magnetic field. In this metaphor, "magnetic north" represents the "pulls" of the world—personal desires, temptations of the flesh, and shifting cultural morals that influence one's destination and legacy.

This image encourages us to prioritize Christ's lordship over temporary pulls, ensuring that our steps lead toward Him as the ultimate destination. To get where you truly want to go, I urge you to start reading the Bible for the first time—or read it more every day if you have already embraced this Jesus.

The Gospel of John is an excellent place to start. An easy-to-read translation, such as the English Standard Version (ESV) or the New International Version (NIV), can be helpful.

Regularly reading God's Word brings closeness and clarity about who you are in Christ. As Oswald Chambers noted in *My Utmost for His Highest*, "The great secret joy is that you are rightly related to Jesus."

Jesus was—and is—a proven historical figure who lived a perfect life, spoke perfect truth, and was tortured and killed because He threatened the religious and political status quo. But He conquered death and rose from the grave, a fact confirmed by hundreds of witnesses.

If we claim eternal life through Him, a transcendent hope becomes ours. What cost Him everything is available to us as a gift—a gift with no strings attached. No reasonable person can deny that if Jesus' teachings were lived out today, the world would be a far better place. His Word calls us to:

- Listen until you truly hear and understand (Proverbs 18:13).
- Be quick to listen, slow to speak, and slow to anger (James 1:19).
- Give generously (Proverbs 21:26).
- Pray without ceasing (Luke 6:38).
- Answer without harsh words (Proverbs 15:1).
- Speak the truth in love (Ephesians 4:15).
- Do everything without grumbling or arguing (Philippians 2:14).
- Understand that love always protects and always trusts (1 Corinthians 13:7).

- Forgive as the Lord has forgiven us (Colossians 3:13).
- Avoid promising what we can't deliver (Proverbs 22:26-27).

Jesus unlocks true greatness within us when we move beyond personal success and offer what we have learned to comfort, encourage, and inspire others. It's kind of like one of my favorite lines from a song by Big Daddy Weave: **"It was the kindness of Jesus that drew me in . . . to tell you my story is to tell of Him."**

That is a legacy worth aspiring to.

I love how the Bible consistently teaches that God is omnipresent—He is everywhere at all times—and that nothing escapes His notice. In that sense, God is always "watching" us, but not in a frightening, Big Brother-style way. Instead, He sees all and misses nothing:

> The eyes of the Lord are everywhere, keeping watch on the wicked and the good.
>
> —Proverbs 15:3 (NIV)

> Nothing in all creation is hidden from God's sight. Everything is uncovered and laid bare before the eyes of him to whom we must give account.
>
> —Hebrews 4:13 (NIV)

> "For my eyes are on all their ways. They are not hidden from me, nor is their iniquity concealed from my eyes."
>
> —Jeremiah 16:17 (ESV)

So here we are, in my final chapter of *Are You Ready?* It's decision time. Scripture often describes this as a crossroads—a moment of choosing between two fundamentally different paths. Two roads. Two destinations.

You can take the broad road—life apart from Christ, ending in separation from God when you die. Or you can choose the narrow road—and receive eternal life in Christ. Jesus put it this way:

> "Enter by the narrow gate. For the gate is wide and the way is easy that leads to destruction, and those who enter by it are many. For the gate is narrow and the way is hard that leads to life, and those who find it are few."
>
> —MATTHEW 7:13-14 ESV

When you declare your allegiance to Jesus, you will discover a faith that can withstand any circumstance. Your faith will walk you through heartbreak and ambiguity in a fallen world that will remain broken until Jesus returns to restore it.

Even now, you still have the opportunity to turn away from the world's falsehoods and live a life of *perfect imperfection*—a life that makes meaningful contributions along the way. When you are with Him and in Him, and He is in you, the greatest joy and love you will ever experience will grow deeper and richer every day, forever.

Allow Him to open the eyes of your heart to see that He still has everything under control—even the most painful parts of your journey—as the apostle Paul reminds us in one of the most significant passages in Scripture:

> I am convinced that neither death nor life, neither angels nor demons, neither the present nor the future, nor any powers, neither height nor depth, nor anything

> else in all creation, will be able to separate us from the love of God that is in Christ Jesus our Lord.
>
> —Romans 8:38-39 (NIV)

I had the sublime experience of officiating the wedding of my grandson, John Schreckengaust, and his bride, Savannah. When they asked me to bring Jesus into the ceremony, I was glad to do so.

At one point, as their eyes shifted from one another and met mine, I asked them to look past me and, in their mind's eye, visualize the Cross on Calvary. I spoke about the importance of keeping that image in the periphery of their vision throughout their married life.

All of life's deepest questions find their answers in the three years of Jesus' public ministry and in His death on the Cross. When we are "melted existentially" by the acknowledgement of His sacrifice, as pastor Tim Keller, founder of Redeemer Church, said in a sermon one time, we are transformed. Because perfect love and justice collided on the Cross, a way home to eternal salvation was opened for us.[2]

God calls us through His Son to a faith that can withstand all circumstances, and He promises to finish what He has started:

> And I am sure of this, that he who began a good work in you will bring it to completion in the day of Jesus Christ.
>
> —Philippians 1:6 (ESV)

I'm reminded of something a dear friend of mine, Dan Gillespie, said to me shortly before he died a few years ago: **"You cannot**

2 I highly recommend that you check out the Gospel in Life app, which provides access to sermons, devotionals, and resources from Pastor Tim Keller, who passed away in 2023 and is with Jesus now.

make God love you any more than He already does."[3]

God loves us because love is who God is (1 John 4:18), not because of who we are. The sun doesn't shine because the planets deserve light; it shines because that's what a sun does. God loves because that is His very nature.

Consider this insight from British author and theologian C.S. Lewis:

> God loves you not because you are lovable, but because He is the kind of God who loves the unlovable—otherwise He wouldn't be God, He'd just be a bigger version of us.

Which brings me to *the* most critical question in this book: **If you were to die today, are you ready to meet Jesus?**

I know I'm being blunt, but it's a question that must be asked. We are all coming to the end of the road at some point—perhaps sooner than we think.

As you consider your relationships, your view of yourself, your work, and, most importantly, your future, ask yourself this: Who—or what—are you going to hitch your wagon to? I urge you to give this serious thought because death is a day closer today than it was yesterday.

Jesus spoke directly about being ready, watchful, and prepared for the moment to meet Him when we die. Listen to His clear commands:

> "Therefore, stay awake, for you do not know on what

3 Dan and his wife, Kristen, founded a wonderful ministry, that helps at-risk children in the southeastern African country of Malawi. The website can be found at miqlat.com.

day your Lord is coming . . . Therefore you also must be ready, for the Son of Man is coming at an hour you do not expect."

MATTHEW 24:42-44 (ESV)

"Watch therefore, for you know neither the day nor the hour."

—MATTHEW 25:13 (ESV) at the conclusion of the Parable of the Ten Virgins

"Be on guard, keep awake. For you do not know when the time will come . . . What I say to you I say to all: Stay awake."

—MARK 13:33-37 (ESV)

"Stay dressed for action and keep your lamps burning . . . Blessed are those servants whom the master finds awake when he comes . . . You also must be ready, for the Son of Man is coming at an hour you do not expect."

—LUKE 12:35-40 (ESV)

There is no second chance to get right with God after you draw your last breath. Each of us will stand personally before Jesus and give an account of our lives. That meeting is unavoidable—and final.

There are only two possible outcomes:

- **Those who have come to know and have accepted Jesus Christ**—forgiven and reconciled—will be welcomed into heaven with joy and eternal life.
- **Those who have rejected Jesus** and are not in Him will face condemnation and separation from

God—and that lasts forever.

Don't let the world distract you with endless activity or the pursuit of material "stuff." Don't settle for temporary pleasures that undermine a legacy that truly matters.

I sincerely hope you're ready to meet Jesus after you die because that moment will be the best thing that will ever happen to you. Nothing else comes close because we're talking about eternity—as in forever.

Be ready to meet Him!

How much time do any of us really have left? Only God knows. And remember: you don't get to spend anyone else's time.

John Hiatt, one of my favorite singer-songwriters, captured this reality bluntly in his song, "Slow Turning."

> Time is short, and here's the damn thing about it
> You're gonna die, gonna die for sure . . .
> You can learn to live with love or without it
> But there ain't no cure

To love and to be loved—these two treasured and pressing human desires are continuously and eternally available in Jesus. He's there for you, waiting.

When you place your trust in Christ, then you have the correct approach to answering my thesis question: "Are you ready?" Your future with Him is secure, even though your life remains a work in progress.

You're like a child riding in the back seat of a car. The child doesn't need to know the route home or keep one eye on the road; the one who loves him is driving. In the same way, when your trust rests in Christ, you are traveling in the right direction, on the right road. Sure, you will encounter potholes—even breakdowns—but you will arrive at the right destination.

If you are not yet a follower of Jesus, my prayer is that you will feel the urgency to investigate the truth of the Gospel, recognizing that you were created to have a relationship with God. Get to know this Jesus:

> "Fear not, for I am with you;
> be not dismayed, for I am your God;
> I will strengthen you, I will help you,
> I will uphold you with my righteous right hand."
>
> —Isaiah 41:10 (ESV)

If you *have* placed your trust in Jesus, now is the time to draw closer and go deeper. Let Jesus be your everything, and you will live more ready than you could have ever imagined. All of Him in all of you. A weary world is waiting to see your daily reflection of the one thing that matters most.

Life is an adventure. Your adventure—your story—is being written and read by those you encounter every day.

It takes courage to commit to a life of faith in Jesus, which reminds me of one of the most iconic and memorable lines from the 2001 film *The Princess Diaries*, which came out when our youngest daughter, Gigi, was nine years old. The emotional heart of the film came when Clarisse stated, "Courage is not the absence of fear but the judgment that something is more important than fear."

That line of dialogue made such an impression on me that I had it printed and framed on Gigi's dresser for her to look at and consider as she grew up.

Yet even that remarkable line doesn't hold a candle to what

may be the most encouraging verse in Scripture:

> "What no eye has seen, nor ear heard
> nor the heart of man imagined,
> what God has prepared for those who love him."
>
> —1 CORINTHIANS 2:9 (ESV)

How many of us have looked inside ourselves with courage? To own and not just know the faith that will stand, no matter what, requires a power beyond our own for our personal victory. He is knocking and waiting for you to open the door (Revelation 3:20-21).

We have no idea what heaven will be like. Nobody has come back with a verified GoPro tour recap. We have hopes, ideas, and guesses, but whatever God has prepared for us is beyond what our finite minds can fully imagine.

Sometimes, you just have to go for it.

That's my attitude today and the attitude I needed when I found myself in the lineup off a small island in the South Pacific known as Tavarua, near Fiji's main island of Viti Levu.

Tavarua is a heart-shaped island with just twenty-nine acres and surrounded by a coral reef. There are seven surfing breaks, but the most famous is Cloudbreak, a powerful left that breaks over a razor-sharp coral reef and is ranked as one of the best waves in the world—and one of the most intimidating.

Naturally, Cloudbreak is where I wanted to surf the minute I arrived from California. This would have been in the late '80s, when I was in my mid-thirties.

After checking into a rustic surf camp, I slipped into my trunks and pulled my surfboard from its padded travel bag as the sun dipped low. I needed a panga to take me out to the open-ocean break, located about a mile and a half south of the Tavarua Island.

I rode a panga like this one (pictured from a surfing trip to Indonesia) when I got my first look at the world-renowned surfing spot called Cloudbreak, a good mile off the coast of Tavarua, a small island in the South Pacific near Fiji's main island of Viti Levu. Cloudbreak was pumping that day . . . and I was nervous.

Cloudbreak's left-hand barrels had a reputation for being epic fun and typically ranged in size from four to six feet. As our small boat drew closer, though, I could see that the surf was pumping at ten to twelve feet. Not exactly the "warm-up" session I was hoping for.

Two questions immediately came to mind: *Am I ready for this? Can I drop in?* A failed takeoff or bailout would be risky and could drag me across the shallow, sharp coral reef.

Waiting in the lineup, legs dangling in crystal blue water in the low eighties, I told myself that I hadn't come all this way to sit on my board in the South Pacific. I maneuvered myself into position, and when a massive wave began to crest, I paddled hard and dropped in.

I came out of my bottom turn and settled into a barrel so large that you could have driven a VW bus through it. I will never forget looking ahead and seeing a pinhole of sunlight at the end of the wave. I was beyond stoked as I stayed crouched in the pipe. This was momentary perfection on planet Earth—

. . . until Mother Nature swatted me mercilessly.

In a nanosecond, I lost my balance and wiped out. I was tossed around like a rag doll, the wave's power feeling like I'd been hit by a freight train.

Despite the violent thrashing, I somehow avoided any deep gashes and cuts . . . so I was okay when I popped to the surface. The only bad news was that my board snapped in two.

Even so, I've never regretted dropping in. Not only was I rewarded with the largest liquid cavern I'd ever dared enter, but having the guts to take off was a defining moment of growth for me. The pure, boundless joy I felt that late afternoon still fills the memory crevices of my heart.

Cloudbreak's waves are so powerful that my surfboard was no match when I wiped out on my first—and most memorable—wave. I'm glad I brought a backup board with me for the rest of that epic trip.

I know an even greater inexpressible joy awaits me when I take my final breath. Jesus will be there, extending His arms and gathering me close to Him. As an often bumbling, knuckleheaded everyman, I remain forever humbly and gratefully confident that I will hear Him say those wonderful words: "Well done, good and faithful servant. You have been faithful over a little; I will set you over much. Enter into the joy of your master" (Matthew 25:21, ESV).

There will be moments for us all when life's dots connect, and everything feels right with the world. In those moments, the song in your heart, the sunset before your eyes, or the unexplainable love you feel will grow into an eternal chorus of glory, drawing you home to a joy that will never, ever end.

When your heart, mind, and soul stir within you, lean into that door that has cracked open, letting the light spill through. Step forward and go through it to be embraced by the name above all names, Jesus Christ:

> Therefore God has highly exalted him and bestowed on him the name that is above every name, so that at the name of Jesus every knee should bow, in heaven and on earth and under the earth, and every tongue confess that Jesus Christ is Lord, to the glory of God the Father.
>
> —PHILIPPIANS 2:9-11 (ESV)

So, I'll ask one final time: **Are you ready to drop in—and be assured of the same inexpressible joy when you finally meet Him face to face?**

May your answer be an all-the-way yes!

Praise be Jesus Christ!

Afterword

Whether you are considering committing yourself to Jesus for the first time or recommitting, these next few moments and words will make all the difference.

If you truly desire to be ready to meet the One who created you, then say the following prayer out loud and let the words sink into the deepest recesses of your grateful heart as you start to live a life of readiness:

> Dearest Jesus, I cannot go on in this life without You any longer. I admit I am a sinner and that I need You as my Savior. I am sorry for all the wrong choices I have made, and I desire to be on the one true trajectory towards You. I believe You died for my sins and rose from the dead. I invite You into my heart today, and I commit to following You for the rest of my life. I pray this in Your holy and precious name—Jesus. Amen.

If you have said these words and need further encouragement or direction, please email me at jay@jcgdev.com or call or text me at 858-204-5438. I will respond.

Be blessed and be encouraged today!

Photo Gallery

Family photos are touching because they do far more than capture faces and places—they freeze fleeting moments of connection, love, joy, vulnerability, and shared history. What great memories attending a Padres baseball game with son-in-law Scott and two of my grandsons, River and Will, or looking for sea creatures when the tide was ultra-low in Santa Barbara.

A great family shot overlooking the beach in Carlsbad, California: from the left, our son, Michael, me, Catherine, our daughter Amber, her husband Scott, our grandson John, and John's wife, our granddaughter-in-law Savannah. Below left, our grown-up grandson Will and Catherine ham it up.

Our daughter, Georgiana, who goes by Gigi, is on the autism spectrum. She has faced unique challenges over her thirty-three years, but she continuously makes us proud and has taught us all to approach life with a Christ-centered, joy-filled heart despite the obstacles she faces every day.

In the bottom-right photo, our eldest grandson, John, lovingly hugs his siblings, Grace and Will, and his cousins, River and Sage (Michael's kids), in the Rocky Mountain resort town of Telluride, Colorado.

Ditties, Poems, and Prayers

by Jay Wentz

The following are some ditties, poems, and prayers that came to me along the journey of writing *Are You Ready?* I hope some may inspire you as they did me.

Wonderful Father
Precious Son
Holy Spirit
Against Thee stand none

■

You have promised to get me through
Help me leave behind what is not of You

■

Please transform me, Father, and set me free
For the rest of my life, I commit to Thee

■

It's never wrong to finish strong

■

On the road to glory
Lay your defenses down
Don't be the roadblock you've become
Since you've been carrying it around
There's a feeling stirring up inside
Comes from a place outside of you
You can still grab what's familiar
Or you can finally break on through
A fire sparks within you
In a place you've never known
But in an eternal moment
You know you're headed home

■

Though foreboding lurks around me
And tremble is in the air
The weight of the world is crushing
But I do not despair
For You have promised good to me
Plans to prosper from time before
I'll trust in You to see me through
Now and forever more

■

If they see something good in me
Thank you, Jesus, for it is Thee
Now I see my way clear
I no longer live in fear
Now I fully trust in You

■

The world is such a great big place
And I fill such a small, small space
But my space is filled with thoughts of You
My rock, my fortress, my east from west
With each breath, I offer You my best
The trials will come this year, I know
But in the valley, downtrodden and low
I will remember what You did for me
All will be well, my heart set free

▪

Dear sweet Jesus, may all of me
Be for all of You this day

▪

ABIDE
Always
Believe
In
Divine
Eminence

▪

What kind of love is this
That You should die for me?
To leave Your riches, the eternal King
And be crucified on a tree
Pierced and scorned, misunderstood
Your only desire was to show true good
Your words, Your life, Your tender care
While You walked Your earth, they filled the air
He revealed himself and what true love is

And now we have what is His
I have tried to be grateful
I have tried to be good
I have tried to do all
That I know I should
I have trusted You, Jesus
Because of Your precious blood
You have seen me through
No matter the flood
I am so sorry for those times
When I let you down
My tears, they fall without reprieve·
And on my head, You still place a crown
My heart is Yours
As Your heart is mine
Eternity links us
Forever entwined

■

The dam is broken
There is a flood
Over me flows
His redemptive blood
What was built up
Needed to go
What was high
Was meant to be low
Heart and soul pierced
Like on the tree
My true self beckons
I've been set free
Sometimes there is nothing to say
What you thought you were saving

You lost anyway
My Lord and Savior
How clear I now see
I surrender all
I lift my hands to Thee
My tears I offer
Every breath as well
For You have saved me
From the gates of hell

■

Thank you, God, for everything
Thank you for the birds that sing
Thank you for the joy You bring
Thank you, God, for everything

Acknowledgements

Writing *Are You Ready?* has been a passion of mine for many years, during which I studied, thought, and prayed about various ideas that God placed in my heart, soul, and mind. One could say that the thoughts and discoveries I explore in *Are You Ready?* stem from my spiritual journey through my years on this Earth, which I've tried to express in this book.

Let's face it: many of our life experiences powerfully influence who we are as individuals. A significant portion of our makeup comes from our personal interactions with others—the people God puts in our path. They often influence our thoughts, ideas, or even the direction our lives take.

In a world where a continuous marketing machine entices us each day to grasp at things we are told will add true and lasting meaning to our lives, I hope the timeless truths in God's Word will spur us to be ready to meet Him someday—and leave a legacy that matters. To have one's eyes opened to something far greater—to feel the scales fall at various times along the way—is both marvelous and humbling, as well as a reminder that His mercies are truly new every morning.

Although I can't acknowledge everyone who impacted me along the way, I would like to remember the multitude who have played a role in shaping me. I'll begin with my precious wife, Catherine, a life treasure like none other. Catherine has helped me realize many important things, starting with the importance and beauty of reveling in the ordinary and fast-moving moments of life. She has helped make me a better man along the way.

My mom, Phyllis Wentz, taught me Scrabble at a very young age and gave me a love for words that only grew over time. I'm grateful to my father, Jim Wentz, for instilling a strong work ethic in me.

I would not be where I am today without the love of my immediate family: my daughter Amber and her husband, Scott, and their kids, John, Grace, and Will; my son Michael, and his kids, River and Sage; my daughter, Gigi; my sisters Jan and Julie; and my late brother John.

I also want to acknowledge that there are friends, pastors, and colleagues over many years who may not be aware that many of my thoughts have come from listening to them or our interactions.

Mike Yorkey, my editor and co-writer and now a good friend, showed great patience and shared his years of insight as he helped me write *Are You Ready?* over a five-year span.

Finally, I want to thank my wonderful Father, His precious Son, and the Holy Spirit for breathing life into me and opening my eyes to the wonder of Jesus when He walked this Earth.

When the great love displayed on the Cross at Calvary becomes the bedrock of our reality, everything within us changes for the better . . . and forever. And when that happens, you and I will be ready to meet Him!

About the Authors

Jay Wentz, a lawyer and real estate developer for more than forty years, grew up in the Los Angeles suburb of Sierra Madre until his sophomore year in high school when his family moved to the coastal city of San Clemente, where he fell in love with surfing.

After graduating from San Diego State University, Jay earned a law degree from the University of San Diego and ventured into his first real estate development deals.

Jay and his wife, Catherine, have three children, five grandchildren, and one great-grandchild.

Jay has journaled for fifty years but never set out to write a book until now, laboring to share his thoughts about the things that matter most—life here on Earth and the afterlife. He likes to say that *Are You Ready?* is his love letter to his Lord and Savior, Jesus Christ, to whom he eagerly and often confesses that, without Him, life would have no meaning and be hopeless.

It's his hope and prayer that readers of *Are You Ready?* will be blessed by the power and glory of this incredible Being and draw closer to Him before they take their last breath.

Jay can be contacted at jay@jcgdev.com or by calling or texting him at 858- 204-5438. Please visit his website at AreYouReadyforJesus.com.

Mike Yorkey is a veteran author, editor, and collaborator, and *Are You Ready?* is his 125th book in print. Mike is also the co-author of the internationally bestselling *Every Man's Battle* series with Steve Arterburn and Fred Stoeker.

He and his wife, Nicole, are the parents of two adult children and make their home in Encinitas, California. His website is mikeyorkey.com.

Mike had this to say about collaborating with Jay: "The overarching goal of *Are You Ready?* is to equip readers with an approach to life and its countless questions of readiness. That way, when they close their eyes for the last time, they can rest resolutely confirmed that Jesus was the very reason for their existence."

Made in the USA
Coppell, TX
12 June 2026

81379454R00132